STAYING TENDER

STAYING TENDER

contemplation, pathway to compassion

LUKE BELL O.S.B.

ANGELICO PRESS

First published in the USA
by Angelico Press 2020
Copyright © Luke Bell O.S.B. 2020

For information, address:
Angelico Press, Ltd.
169 Monitor St.
Brooklyn, NY 11222
www.angelicopress.com

978-1-62138-538-7 pb
978-1-62138-539-4 cloth
978-1-62138-540-4 ebook

Book and cover design
by Michael Schrauzer
Cover image: Joel Whybrew

μείνατε ἐν ἐμοί, κἀγὼ ἐν ὑμῖν.

CONTENTS

INTRODUCTION

In my salad days when I was green in judgment I paid very little attention to the interior life, except perhaps as something to be avoided for fear of what might come up out of the depths. But there was one barely noticeable mental habit — hardly more than a tic of the mind — that survived from religious formation that I had received as a teenager. I had been taught it as an "arrow prayer" and, although I didn't pray, sometimes the words would repeat themselves in my mind: "Dwell in me and I in thee." It is an extraordinary grace and gift of God that somehow He got me back. Maybe, just maybe, it was those words that let Him in. I want to share with you some thoughts about them. When I first began to consider them I thought this was my idea. Now I realize it is His. So this book is His, not at all as sharing in His perfection, but simply because it is written as an offering of love for Him, for He is my life.

Its aim is to help you to become prayerfully rooted in what is eternal, and so be a source of compassion. It draws its inspiration chiefly from St John's gospel, written by the disciple loved by the Lord. I hope that will help you to identify with John and know yourself as loved by the Lord. In such a friendship there is a security that helps us to keep steady in a changing world and also to have a heart steadfastly open to others. My meditation on this friendship begins with a consideration of the enduring role of the beloved disciple who is the exemplar of the contemplative. It goes on to consider what it is to share the Lord's life, and what it means for us to abide in Him and He in us. It reflects on the sacramental embodiment of this in the Eucharist and on the sacrifice He offered on the cross. Finally it ponders the maturity of a life lived from the eternal and its full realization in our heavenly homeland.

It is structured according to the days of the week, with one chapter for each day. The week represents the fullness of creation, as in the account at the beginning of the Bible,[1] and its divinely given variety, as in G. K. Chesterton's novel in which its days are personified with their particular characteristics and sit on "seven great chairs, the thrones of the seven days."[2] The special Christian significance of these days guides this book. It starts therefore on Sunday, the day of the resurrection through which God accomplishes a new creation in Christ, and not on Monday, when people's work week customarily begins. It also considers the old meaning of the days and looks at their ancient association with planetary bodies so that through cosmological symbolism it becomes a journey into the heavens. In looking back like this to the cultural and spiritual context into which the Christian faith was born, we can get a better sense of how it looked when it was fresh, and with that see it afresh. For the ancients, heaven could be seen, not simply thought about. With their eyes we can think about reaching beyond our conceptual grasp. With these words and with the more significant contribution of your prayer and example I want to team up with you so that together we may make that journey for which space and time are given us as opportunity and as symbol, the pilgrimage to the perfect joy beyond space and time.

You can use the book for a week's retreat, reading a chapter a day. The chapters begin with a key passage of Scripture which you could meditate on during the day. They also contain a lot of other scripture which could be singled out for reflection. I have used the King James Version of the Bible. Readers of early drafts of the book have suggested that this might be more difficult for people to get their head around than a modern version, so a word of explanation is in order. I don't want you to get your head around it. I want it to get into your heart. I have chosen this

---

1   Gn 1:1–3.

2   G. K. Chesterton, *The Man Who Was Thursday* (Bristol: Arrowsmith, 1929), 318.

version because it is poetic. T.S. Eliot observed (in connection with Dante) that "genuine poetry can communicate before it is understood."[3] That is to say that what comes through it is more than what the mind can grasp, at least to begin with. It speaks first of all to intuition rather than to any analytical faculty. That in us which sees the whole is touched by the poet's own vision of the whole, its words awakening in us what awoke the words in him or her. Just as an inspiration of the oneness of creation can sometimes come through the beauty of nature, so a sense of the one divine source of all meaning can sometimes be received through poetry. It is the genre of the transcendent. Through it can be heard an echo of the music of eternity. If all this is true of poetry it should be true *a fortiori* of versions of Scripture, which is above all the text through which the transcendent comes to us. If we word it so it reflects back to us the quotidian banalities of our own speech with all the limitations of its vision, reducing in effect what it speaks of to that of which we speak, then we tend to make it tamer than it should be. We risk the complacency of thinking we have mastered it replacing the aspiration that it should master us. I do not mean that a contemporary translation makes blunt Scripture, which is "sharper than any two-edged sword."[4] God's word cannot have its power taken away like that. However, an older version, written when the language was richer and less abstract, is more likely to make us pause before the mystery, to humble us before the numinous, to open us to what comes from beyond. Hence I give you these old words. In fact the main argument depends on the Greek text of the New Testament. If that is all Greek to you, I trust you will nonetheless be able to follow my thinking through what I have written.

For reasons similar to the above, this book contains some poetry (including Dante) which can be held receptively in the heart and I hope communicates more than can be immediately

---

3 T.S. Eliot, *Dante*, 2nd edition (London: Faber and Faber Ltd, 1965), 8.

4 Heb 4:12. Scripture citations are from the King James Version of the Bible unless otherwise noted.

grasped. It is probably best not to hurry through its chapters. Rather let it, and particularly the Scripture and poetry in it, slow down your normal pace of reading. If you do not have a week in which to make a retreat, you could read the chapters on seven consecutive Sundays, or over the seven weeks of Easter. Read it in whatever way inspiration suggests to you.

The word "contemplation" comes from the Latin *contemplatio* and that word, more anciently, came from *templum*, meaning a space cut out for augury with its divining of mysteries, the prefix *con* having an intensifying force.[5] It is good to have a place for communing with the sacred, be it only a corner of a room with an icon and a candle. People vary in what they find helpful. An obvious place is a church, but I know people who prefer their private room, or find it helpful to walk slowly while praying, and even someone who has found a cave hidden in a forest in which to put a crucifix and contemplate. The cave especially, but all of these places, are a symbolic expression of the human heart. Perhaps this is what the Lord meant when He said, "When thou prayest, enter into thy closet, and when thou hast shut thy door, pray to thy Father which is in secret."[6] I don't think we can suppose that He was trying to put us off going to church, rather that the motive should not be to "be seen of men."[7] It is a matter of praying from where we are most in earnest, from the heart and not from the fancies that flit across the brain. A special place and some sort of solitude help this.

In our day and age, however, it is not so much a matter of marking off a place as marking off a time. Anciently, before the Gadarene rush towards the Apocalypse (the restless, caffeine-fueled, sleep-deprived drive to master time which ends by trampling it underfoot as though it were not a gift) had really got underway and there was a stillness in the cycle of the seasons, the sense of the sacred was first of all identified with place,

5 https://www.etymonline.com/word/contemplation
6 Mt. 6:6.   7 Mt. 6:5.

as with the *templum*. Now our spiritual condition demands taking time out: time not given to planning for another time, speculating about the future, raking over the past. This is rather time that would sacrifice itself, time received and given back, so that it might be transcended, so that — if only "through a glass, darkly"[8] — we might glimpse what is beyond, so that we might be open to eternity.

The book has been written from within a cloistered life and while I am happy with the thought that it might be read by those so enclosed it is truly meant for everyone. There is no concern that you need to fit a particular niche. Love of the Lord is what matters; love of the Lord is all that gives these words any value, and who am I to say that there may not be more love of the Lord in getting the children off to school than in getting to Lauds? I write about contemplation, but contemplation is not about abandoning one's duties to have more leisure; it is about the source of our life, about living from what is eternal rather than from what is temporal, about living in a dwelling "founded upon a rock."[9] In other words, it is about living from love rather than from narrow self-interest. That is not quantifiable in terms of what you do or where you do it. To put it metaphorically, you can either change a light bulb standing on a chair balanced on a table not big enough to take all its legs or you can use a proper stepladder. To live and act merely for considerations relating to what is going to (or might) happen further on in time is like the former arrangement: it is inherently unstable. To live and act on the basis of eternity is like doing the work from a stepladder: the arrangement won't collapse and it brings us a bit nearer to heaven. The issue is not how many light bulbs are changed, or even what is done, it is the relationship with the Living and Eternal Lord, the True Light. Some pause is generally helpful to establish this and I offer you here a context for such a pause. If I have made of my entire remaining life such a pause, that reflects

8 1 Co 13:12.   9 Mt 7:25.

my call, not yours. I ask not that you share my way of life, only that in your charity you remember me in your friendship with the Lord of love.

Dom Luke Bell
@domlukebell
Feast of Saint John the Divine, 2019

CHAPTER ONE

the disciple Jesus loved

SUNDAY, DAY FOR CONTEMPLATION

> *"Then Peter, turning about, seeth the disciple
> whom Jesus loved following; which also leaned
> on his breast at supper, and said, Lord, which is
> he that betrayeth thee? Peter seeing him saith to
> Jesus, Lord, and what shall this man do? Jesus
> saith unto him, If I will that he tarry till I come,
> what is that to thee? follow thou me."*[1]

Let's start with the resurrection. Sunday is the day of the resurrection. It is named for the sun, which was worshiped in the later Roman Empire as *Sol Invictus*, the unconquered sun returning each day and increasing its presence again after the winter solstice, but for Christians it is the day of the return from the dead of Christ, "the light of the world."[2] It is a day for the joy of the resurrection, a day to receive that joy, a day to share that joy—particularly in the celebration of the Eucharist. The resurrection is the central message of the Christian faith. It teaches us that evil and suffering are not the end, but rather the occasion of the planting that comes before a great harvest and that "They that sow in tears shall reap in joy."[3] The resurrection transforms how we handle things of the world, how we relate to others, how we experience sorrow and loss. Because we know that life is more than we can see, because we are convinced that we can never truly lose it, because we are oriented to the vision

---

1 Jn 21:20–23.   2 Jn 8:12, 9:5.   3 Ps 126:5.

1

of the "pure river of water of life, clear as crystal, proceeding out of the throne of God and of the Lamb,"[4] we rejoice. We stand in the dawn of the resurrection, welcoming newness of life, open to the divine life ever ancient, ever new. That is an openness to what is beyond our knowing, a readiness to relate to what does not pass away, a refusal to be shut in by what does pass away.

The Apostle to the Apostles, the first witness to the resurrection, sees the sign that we are not limited to a life that has to end, to what our earthly formulations present to us, to what is merely temporal: "The first day of the week cometh Mary Magdalene early, when it was yet dark, unto the sepulchre, and seeth the stone taken away from the sepulchre."[5] A contemporary poet envisages the moment:

> Light pours into this volcanic cave
> through a glancing crack in brightly whitewashed stone
> heady rays from the desert heights above
> blaze in this emptiness we jointly own
> where we have come to learn the name of love
> and are therefore at last, at last, alone[6]

"Light" is the light of the risen Christ; the "crack" is the fissure in our notions received from time and space; the "heights above" are the divine transcendence; the "emptiness" is the freedom from egoism; "love" is what this makes possible; being "alone" is the oneness of mutual indwelling. How do we make all of this our own? The way is shown to us by the two Apostles to whom Mary Magdalene goes:

> Then she runneth, and cometh to Simon Peter, and
> to the other disciple, whom Jesus loved, and saith
> unto them, They have taken away the Lord out of the

4 Rv 22:1.   5 Jn 20:1.
6 "Magdalene" in *Love's Many Names: Poems by Sam Davidson* (Brooklyn, NY: Angelico Press, 2018), 26.

sepulchre, and we know not where they have laid him. Peter therefore went forth, and that other disciple, and came to the sepulchre. So they ran both together: and the other disciple did outrun Peter, and came first to the sepulchre. And he stooping down, and looking in, saw the linen clothes lying; yet went he not in. Then cometh Simon Peter following him, and went into the sepulchre, and seeth the linen clothes lie, And the napkin, that was about his head, not lying with the linen clothes, but wrapped together in a place by itself. Then went in that other disciple, which came first to the sepulchre, and he saw and believed.[7]

In one sense the most important phrase here is "whom Jesus loved." That is because the journey into the eternal begins with love, specifically an awareness of being loved by the Lord: "Herein is love, not that we loved God; but that he loved us."[8] John shows all of us who we are: people loved by Jesus. It is that awareness of being loved that leads him to run faster. It enables him to stoop down and look into the place of revelation. It is an awareness of this love that is at the heart of contemplative life. It is also necessary to go into the place of revelation, to go where love draws us, and Peter models that. He gives the lead, active in his commitment. It is however John who sees and believes: he is the contemplative who perceives the meaning of what he beholds. Close to the Lord, he understands. He looks into the tomb and sees that "the light shineth in the darkness; and the darkness comprehended it not."[9] According to St Augustine, John's gospel is contemplative, the other gospels are active. Tradition tells us that Mark's gospel draws on the recollections of Peter. In Mark, the action moves more swiftly than in the others. Words like "immediately" and "straitway" echo through it.[10] Although its

---

7　Jn 20:2–8.　　　8　1 Jn 4:10.　　　9　Jn 1:5.
10　For example: Mk 1:10, 12, 18, 20, 21, 28.

final verses are thought by scholars to be from another hand, they fit with this emphasis on activity since the gospel culminates in active proclamation: "And they went forth, and preached everywhere, the Lord working with them, and confirming the word with signs following."[11] That proclamation too is part of being with the Lord, but first we need to contemplate what He reveals. That is a reason why the Christian week begins with Sunday.

Staying in the Light

As well as being the day of the resurrection, Sunday is the day of the sun, symbol of resurrection, sign of "the tender mercy of our God; whereby the dayspring from on high hath visited us, to give light to them that sit in darkness and in the shadow of death, to guide our feet into the way of peace."[12] This book is about that "tender mercy of our God," about how to be in the place where it is received, open to it. This is exactly the same as how to be in the place where it is given, for it is always given to one open to it. It is about how to stay in that place, which is exactly the same as how to be in the place where God stays. "God is light"[13] and so it is about how to stay in the place of light, which is the place of peace since there all sufferings are as so many precious sapphires,[14] just as the darkness of outer space appears celestially blue when looked at from where the sun is shining. That blue symbolizes the beauty of the peace the one who is light-filled has even when faced with troubles.[15] It is about how to stay tender; how to keep loving when the wounded heart is inclined to shut itself away; how to make of the tenderness of the heart's very wounds a tenderness that is a compassion open to all human distress. This book is about how to stay in God; it is about how to stay in God with the staying power of the Omnipotent; ultimately, it is about how to stay in God in the bliss of eternal joy.

11 Mk 16:20.   12 Lk 1:78–79.   13 1 Jn 1:5.
14 The idea of suffering as something precious is developed in Chapter 6.
15 This is further developed in my book *The Meaning of Blue* (Brooklyn: Angelico Press, 2014), 40–42.

Concomitantly, therefore, it is about staying in the vital heart of the tradition which St Paul wrote of as having been "received of the Lord."[16] Like every Christian, I too have received this tradition of Christ's gift of Himself and so hear in it the words of the Lord: "freely ye have received, freely give."[17] So I write this to pass on the tradition. You might ask, "Can I not read it in the old books?" Yes, you can; but to be vital a tradition needs a heart and soul alive in the time in which it has to live. So I seek to be not just a channel but an artery in the body of Christ through which can flow the tradition's "precious lifeblood" so that it might be "treasured up on purpose to a life beyond life."[18]

The tradition lives in time and it lives in the week, in which particular days have special meanings for Christians, such as that already mentioned of Sunday. These contribute to the pattern of the book. Also underpinning the book is an understanding that came from the intellectual and cultural soil in which the Christian tradition grew. If this is now for the most part what C.S. Lewis called a "discarded image,"[19] that is no reason to reject what it can offer by way of poetic intuition, to say the least. That such an image is related to spiritual reality is suggested by the recorded words of the nineteenth-century visionary Blessed Anne Catherine Emmerich.[20] The image is formed from what we can see in the sky. In question is "the invisible things" of God "being understood by the things that are made."[21] Just as, anciently, the blue sky of the day spoke of heaven, so the night sky spoke of the immutable. What was on earth, styled as "sublunary," was changeable, what belonged to the seven spheres that surrounded the earth and were marked by the sun, the moon and the five visible planets was beyond the flux that troubles this mortal life. Here were peace and harmony. It is to this—even though the full harmony does not reach

---

16 1 Cor 11:23.   17 Mt 10:8.   18 John Milton, *Areopagitica*.
19 C.S. Lewis, *The Discarded Image* (Cambridge University Press, 1964).
20 Anne Catherine Emmerich, *Inner Life & Worlds of Soul & Spirit* (Brooklyn: Angelico Press, 2018), 87–92.   21 Rom 1:20.

them — that Lorenzo, in Shakespeare's *The Merchant of Venice*, asks his beloved to turn her eyes:

> Sit, Jessica. Look how the floor of heaven
> Is thick inlaid with patens of bright gold.
> There's not the smallest orb which thou behold'st
> But in his motion like an angel sings,
> Still quiring to the young-ey'd cherubins;
> Such harmony is in immortal souls;
> But whilst this muddy vesture of decay
> Doth grossly close it in, we cannot hear it.[22]

They are, of course, looking at "the floor of heaven" from underneath. Escaping "this muddy vesture of decay" is an upward journey. For the ancients gazing (like Lorenzo and Jessica) into the heavens revealed the threshold of immortality "thick inlaid with patens of bright gold" and the pathway of the soul to beyond "our bourne of Time and Place."[23] (The word "patens" is used for the plates on which are the Sacred Hosts during Mass and so suggests the specifically Christian point of access to the eternal imaged in the heavens and their spheres.) The outermost sphere, that of Saturn, expressed the nearest antechamber to the timeless and dimensionless eternity of God. That is where this book seeks to lead you. Like each chapter of this book, each of the spheres is associated through its planet with a day of the week: the last, Saturn's, with Saturday. So my aspiration is to be Beatrice to your Dante and lead you into seventh heaven![24]

We start with the sun. Of all the heavenly bodies associated with days of the week, it is the only one that is luminous.[25]

22 *The Merchant of* Venice, Act 5, scene 1, lines 58–65 in *The Riverside Shakespeare* (Boston: Houghton Mifflin Company, 1974), 280.

23 Tennyson, *Crossing the Bar.*

24 *Paradiso,* cantos 21 & 22, in *Dante, The Divine Comedy 3: Paradiso,* Italian text, trans. and comment, John D. Sinclair (Oxford University Press, 1961).

25 Spike Bucklow, *The Alchemy of Paint: Art, Science and Secrets from the Middle Ages* (London: Marion Boyers Publishers Ltd., 2009), 126.

Its light symbolizes the eternal day of God and His universal benevolence, for it rises "on the evil and on the good."[26] It is associated with gold, a metal which does not rust, and so with the imperishable good of "heaven, where neither moth nor rust doth corrupt."[27] Its day celebrates both the creation and the new creation in Christ, the first rest of God upon the completion of the creation and the final rest of His faithful in Christ. The Bible tells us that God blessed and sanctified this day on which He rested[28] and so on Sunday we rest in anticipation of our eternal rest in Him. It is a day to remember that "one thing is needful,"[29] a day to remember what does not pass away, a day for contemplation. Sunday prepares the great work of beholding.

The Beloved of Jesus

The work of beholding is personified in the disciple Jesus loved, the apostle and evangelist John. His symbol is "a flying eagle,"[30] which soars above the earth and, traditionally, looks upon the sun without blinking, as Christ gazes on the glory of God. John is the one who proclaims that as the eagle carries its young to the sun, so we can be borne up to God by Christ. He models contemplation for us. As he was intimate with Christ, so can we be; as he gazed upon His saving work, so can we; as he saw the empty tomb "and believed,"[31] so can we. His name belongs to every contemplative, in the same way that the Lord attributed the name of the prophet Elias to the prophet John the Baptist[32] and in the same way that the name of Peter is attributed by His church to every Pope.

This makes sense of an otherwise rather redundant-seeming passage at the end of the fourth gospel:

> Then Peter, turning about, seeth the disciple whom
> Jesus loved following; which also leaned on his breast

26 Mt 5:45.   27 Mt 620.   28 Gn 2:2–3.   29 Lk 10:42.
30 Rv 4:7.   31 Jn 20:8.   32 Mt 17:12.

at supper, and said, Lord, which is he that betrayeth
thee? Peter seeing him saith to Jesus, Lord, and what
shall this man do? Jesus saith unto him, If I will that
he tarry till I come, what is that to thee? follow thou
me. Then went this saying abroad among the brethren, that that disciple should not die: yet Jesus said
not unto him, He shall not die; but, If I will that he
tarry till I come, what is that to thee?[33]

These words of Jesus asking Peter what business of his it
is if John is still around when He comes appear to have been
recorded merely to clear up a misunderstanding, specific to the
very beginning of the Christian epoch, which interpreted them
as indicating that John was not to die. Yet they are situated just
after the account of resurrection life breaking into our world. In
a gospel full of eternal truth that resonates anew in every age it
is not plausible that its meaning can be limited to clarifying a
detail. It goes beyond this to proclaim that the presence of the
contemplative calling, personified by John, endures for all time,
even until the coming again of the Lord.

The entire weight of the meaning of the passage depends
on the word that is given in this rendering as "tarry" and is
in Greek μένειν (*menein*). The entire weight of the meaning of
this book, which argues that our ability to love depends upon
what it signifies, depends on this word also. And so it needs
some explanation. The word μένειν (*menein*) is variously translated as "abide," "dwell," "stay," "continue," "remain." Translators
of the Bible have had to vary the English word used to render
it, for no one word conveys its full range of meanings. Perhaps
"abide" comes nearest, for it indicates both enduring and living
(as in the cognate "abode," the place where someone lives). It
points to the eternal life to which John's gospel repeatedly refers.
Also indicated by μένειν (*menein*) is that perseverance by which

33 Jn 21:20–23.

one becomes rooted in the eternity of God and so able to enjoy eternal life: to "continue" in this life is to "remain" eternally; to "abide" now in God is finally to "dwell" in everlasting habitations and to be able to live this life as from our home there; to "stay" faithful is to be stayed by the God who is our rock.

Living Seeing

These meanings presuppose the absolute that is God. It is worth reflecting on how the sense of this absolute has slipped from our culture, so as to refocus on it. The truth is that in our time we tend to take for granted a false absolute. The urge of the spirit of our age is to try to make what is here on earth abiding. The outcomes of this approach are not always happy: we have, for example, asbestos which survives fire but is deadly on contact and plastic which survives decay but whose accumulation threatens the survival of the ecosystem. The reaching towards a this-worldly and thus false absolute goes back to the 15th century. At that time the idea arose that the way to depict reality (literally, in painting, and concomitantly conceptually) was a perspective seen from a single point. In paintings (and indeed minds) ordered like this distant things seem smaller, nearer things larger. Further, space envisaged like this can be subjected to mathematical calculation. It is an essentially false perspective for a simple reason: it does not move. In effect, it makes what it sees dead, rather like the duke in Browning's poem *My Last Duchess* who had his wife killed but kept her portrait on his wall. The Duke's concern was that his duchess was gladdened by everything, not just him:

> Sir, 'twas all one! My favour at her breast,
> The dropping of the daylight in the west...

She was grateful to everyone, not just him:

> She thanked men — good! but thanked
> Somehow — I know not how — as if she ranked

> My gift of a nine-hundred-years-old name
> With anybody's gift.

She smiled at everyone, not just him:

> Oh sir, she smiled, no doubt,
> Whene'er I passed her; but who passed without
> Much the same smile?

He was not the center of everything. She engaged with others. His response is deadly:

> This grew; I gave commands;
> Then all smiles stopped together. There she stands
> As if alive.[34]

The portrait he is referring to is kept covered by a curtain except when he draws it: he now has total control over the direction of her glance. His last duchess is, as it were, what nature is to the mentality that began with the perspective school of painting (seeing everything from a single point, one's own view) and became a way of looking that murders to dissect (reducing what is living to what can be quantified and controlled by the observer).

Such a way of looking is atemporal. Time, as Plato observed, is a moving image of eternity. God, who is eternal, contains all that is. The whole of time, containing all that happens, is therefore a presentation of what is, as it were, within God and therefore shows forth in an outward way His eternity. The movement within time images the life of Him through whom all things are made. Only the eternal (divine) perspective itself sees what passes in time as static and that in the sense that it is viewed in its totality, so that its very changes are unchanging. Within time, the static view is a false simulacrum of the divine view and one that, basilisk-like,

---

34 *Browning: Poetical Works 1833–1864* (Oxford University Press, 1970), 368.

makes dead what it looks at. It excludes life and, with it, the One who is the resurrection and the life. It exports the absolute from the eternal and with a methodology like the Duke's tries to fix it in the temporal. This kills the life of the soul as surely as the Duchess is killed. It is only in knowing God as absolute that we live: the Lord in His prayer for us said, "This is life eternal, that they might know thee, the only true God, and Jesus Christ whom thou has sent."[35] That knowing cannot be had in a portrait fixing a perspective on life in this world. It demands a humility beyond the mindset of the Duke, who says, "I choose / Never to stoop."[36] It can only be had now, in turning to God in the particular moment that He is giving us and acknowledging His sovereignty. In that moment we can be present to God just as He will be manifestly present to all of creation at the end of time. If "of that day and that hour knoweth no man"[37] that is in a sense because it does not belong to time at all: it is the eternal reabsorbing time. Yet the eternal is immediately present to us if we turn our soul to it. That presence of the Eternal is vivifying. A gaze of the soul cast over the things of this world with the intention of getting a fixed picture may have some practical uses, but if it is taken to give us the sum of absolute reality it is not vivifying but petrifying.

A static view like this not only excludes the natural mode of perception, which relates to reality by the constant changing of one's point of view as one's eyes move (to say nothing of the doubling of point of view that two eyes give), but also excludes the view of others. More traditional painting iconically depicted other eyes to establish the implication of other seeing. It was fully aware. An icon could communicate not only the sense of others seeing but also the sense of the one looking being seen. So the presence of God is depicted: we are because He sees, for His knowing is our creation. Concomitantly, others' seeing symbolizes His seeing. Each of us participates in His creating through our knowing, but none of us in isolation can have the divinely known whole and living picture. We approach it to the extent that we allow a more-than-one-pair-of-eyes approach. We need others. So other eyes shown in icons depict the communion we have in God, the mutual seeing and loving with Him and with our fellow creatures that leads to life. Just as "faith cometh by hearing,"[38] so we have to accept others' viewpoints from what they say. What they see is invisible to us, just as the true Absolute is invisible. The tendency of our time is to trade the Absolute in for a view we can command and that we can use to control, but the cost is that it is dead and lonely, we are dead lonely, the lonely dead. Recovery of the true and invisible Absolute leads to life and fellowship. To abandon the static view for the moving one is to allow oneself to be moved, to have tender compassion for others. It is also to find a truly stable and secure abode, encompassing all that is, from which one can reach out to them.[39]

Monastic Perseverance

The contemplative tradition is about abiding in this Absolute and finding life therein, a life that is in an open-hearted communion with others in the depth of their being. It is about abiding and it abides. Its practice is characterized by abiding. One of the vows a Benedictine monk takes is that of stability: that he will abide in the monastic life, and normally in one place, for his whole life.[40] It is perseverance in this, not learning or practical skills, that determines if someone can become a Benedictine. St Benedict even recommends keeping aspirants to the life waiting at the door for four or five days to test their perseverance. Even if this is now adapted to contemporary conditions of life, persistence over time is still considered a key indicator of whether someone has a truly godly motivation for undertaking the life.[41]

38 Rom 10:17.

39 This line of thought is indebted to Johannes Hoff, *The Analogical Turn: Rethinking Modernity with Nicholas of Cusa* (Grand Rapids, Michigan/ Cambridge UK: Eerdmans, 2013), especially part II.

40 The Rule of Saint Benedict, Chapter 58.   41 Rule, Chapter 58.

The Rule of St Benedict indicates that the one who has been accepted as a novice should be asked three times over the course of a year if he still wants to abide by its precepts. He is to be tested in all patience.[42] Once he has become a monk he should normally abide in the enclosure of the monastery and things there should be arranged so that as far as is possible all that is needed will be within that enclosure.[43] There are precautions about leaving it: unauthorized eating outside the monastery is prohibited; prayers are to be said for monks who go on a journey and also on their return, when they are not to gossip about what they may have seen or heard outside the monastery; no one is to leave the enclosure without the abbot's permission.[44] All of this is a practical expression of a spiritual truth: that God abides and by abiding in Him we find life and love. As the monastery is the place of worship of God and of prayer — both because of how it is ordered and because of who is there — it represents the New Jerusalem where God is all in all. Abiding there in the right spirit (which is basically not a complaining spirit) is a means of abiding in God.

Of course this is not the only means. The spiritual truth that has its expression in perseverance in the monastery can also be expressed by not abiding anywhere in this world. Mendicant friars are always moving to a new place, always on a pilgrimage, because nothing in this world abides as God abides. While a monk will allow abiding in one place to point beyond itself to abiding in God, a friar will let abiding in God alone teach that "here have we no continuing city, but seek one to come."[45] Spiritually they are identical in their rootedness in God, the one signifying this by being in one place, the other by not being in one place. The created world both shows and conceals the divine and so can speak of it both positively and negatively. It images abiding in God in a settled place of residence; it shows, through those whose lifestyle is itinerant just as their Lord's

42 Rule, Chapter 58.   43 Rule, Chapter 66.   44 Rule, Chapter 67.
45 Heb 13:14.

was, that it cannot offer the absolute abode which is God alone. Pastoral priests, working under a Bishop, live out their abiding in God by being ready to move from parish to parish as the Bishop asks, for their rootedness is not in the particular social arrangement but in their sonship in Christ who is represented by the Bishop. The people they serve, whether they remain in one parish or not, live out their abiding by their commitment to Sunday worship and to their particular calling: their abiding in these is their abiding in God. As each Sunday comes around it is identified with every other Sunday, with the great Sunday of Easter in which we rejoice and are glad, with the eternal day in which God lives and in which we find our rest in Him.

Our Minutes Hasten to Their End

People abide in God in many ways. That abiding abides, because the passing cannot satisfy, whatever technologies are brought to its prediction and control. These can never exclude the unpredictable event, "the black swan,"[46] least of all the greatest of them: the apocalypse. Writers have always been aware that the precious gifts of this life cannot be grasped for keeps. From Villon's "Où sont les neiges d'antan?" (Where are the snows of yesteryear?)[47] to Samuel Beckett's stark, "They give birth astride of a grave, the light gleams an instant, then it's night once more"[48] they have given voice to the impermanence of our life here below. Shakespeare gave it eloquent articulation in this sonnet:

> Like as the waves make towards the pebbled shore,
> So do our minutes hasten to their end,
> Each changing place with that which goes before,
> In sequent toil all forwards do contend.
> Nativity, once in the main of light,
> Crawls to maturity, wherewith being crowned,

---

46 As explained by Nassim Nicholas Taleb in *The Black Swan* and elsewhere.
47 From Villon, "Ballade des dames du temps jadis."
48 From Beckett, *Waiting for Godot*, Act Two.

> Crookèd eclipses 'gainst his glory fight,
> And time that gave doth now his gift confound.
> Time doth transfix the flourish set on youth,
> And delves the parallels in beauty's brow,
> Feeds on the rarities of nature's truth
> And nothing stands but for his scythe to mow.
> And yet to times in hope my verse shall stand,
> Praising thy worth, despite his cruel hand.[49]

Against the three-quatrain account of the devastation of time is marshaled the final couplet offering literary memorialization, echo of the Word who endures forever, but inescapably not that which was lost. Only the remaining, the abiding of God can touch the woundedness of loss and console the heart of those who mourn. Jesus says to the one whom He loves — which is also you, dear reader — I want him to remain. He offers us a share in His eternal abiding: he wants us to abide — μένειν (*menein*) — in Him, to persevere as contemplatives, to dwell in the mansion He has prepared for us.[50] The word μένειν (*menein*) challenges our culture's voracity for the next thing. It is a word that speaks of something that we feel made for but do not find in our passing life. It invites us to the steadfastness of a rock, to be a rock for others, to be strengthened enough to be tender. It is an invitation to sit at the feet of Jesus as did Mary who "heard his word."[51]

The One Thing Needful

She heard Him say, "One thing is needful: and Mary hath chosen that good part."[52] The needful thing is to abide at the feet of Jesus — the needs of the meal service are secondary: true loving service arises from this abiding — and there learn from Him what it is to look lovingly towards "the Father of Lights."[53] To abide in this friendship with Jesus, to look abidingly to the

---

49 Shakespeare, Sonnet 60.   50 Cf Jn 14:2.   51 Lk 10:39.
52 Lk 10:42.   53 Jas 1:17.

One who abides eternally in the abiding power of the Spirit is the foundation of all good work. To be established in it now and enduringly is to be an agent of blessing, an emissary of heaven, to be one of those of whom St John of the Cross wrote: "Heaven is stable and is not subject to generation, and souls of a heavenly nature are stable and not subject to the engendering of desires or of anything else, for in their way they resemble God Who does not move forever."[54] A soul "of a heavenly nature" is stable enough to love others without depending on a return of love, to forgive without expectation of revenge, to worship without need for consolation. Such a soul's smallest spark of love of God, if purified of craving for being paid for it, is of more value to the world than any amount of activity outside of the stabilizing relationship that Mary at the feet of Jesus models for us.[55] A sister in a Carmelite monastery who in her daily two hours of personal prayer has left behind all concern for things that are below, whose life is "hid with Christ in God,"[56] who is for that time no longer wrapped in the words and concepts that we use for "things on the earth"[57] opens the world to an infinite blessing. A Carthusian monk, whose conversations with those outside the monastery have all but ceased, who speaks with his own fellow monks only once a week, who abides for life in the silence of the cloister is, through the Spirit that unites, as close in the depth of his heart to every person on the planet as anyone whoever. These are particular vocations but they are no more than forms of the essential and universal Christian vocation to abide with Jesus worshiping the Father in the power of the Spirit. People in monasteries are as it were the staff of base camps from which missions are undertaken. In one way or another every disciple

54 Maxims on Love, No 27 in *The Collected Works of St. John of the Cross*, trans. Kieran Kavanaugh O.C.D. and Otilio Rodriguez O.C.D. (Washington, DC: Institute of Carmelite Studies, 1979), 676.

55 Cf. *Thérèse de L'Enfant-Jésus et de la Sainte Face: Oeuvres complètes* (Paris: Éditions du Cerf, 1992), 229.

56 Col 3:3.   57 Col 3:2.

of the Lord needs to touch base with Him. Monastic life is an ancient way of doing so that offers a basis for people to make contact with the essential, but there are other ways of finding spiritual rootedness: faithful practice of prayer need not be limited to particular places and times. Yet some sort of fidelity is necessary to the following of the Lord: every Christian is called to a stability from which to look lovingly towards the Most High.

Contemplation is Forever

John remains. He has eternal life, so in that sense the rumor of his not dying is true, yet the Scripture points beyond this to the truth that the contemplative spirit can never die. It is not that this world (the form of which is passing away) sustains it: rather the contemplative spirit is the reason this world is not dead. Souls open to the Divine Artificer, the Creator of all, open the world to its life, the life to which the first letter of John so eloquently witnesses: "That which was from the beginning, which we have heard, which we have seen with our eyes, which we have looked upon, and our hands have handled, of the Word of life; (For the life was manifested, and we have seen it, and bear witness, and shew unto you that eternal life, which was with the Father, and was manifested unto us)."[58] This is nothing less than the life of Him by Whom "all things were made."[59] The world stands because it is connected by such souls to the *nunc stans*, the abiding now of God. The abidingly abiding of souls in the abiding is the source of true life. The chapters that follow explore that life — spoken of by the Lord in His great priestly prayer when He said, "...this is life eternal, that they might know thee the only true God and Jesus Christ, whom thou hast sent"[60] — and how we may dwell steadfastly in it, drawing especially on the gospel and letters of John. Our Lord invites us to be shown, as His disciples, His own enjoyment of it. The next chapter reflects on that.

58 1 Jn 1:1–2.   59 Jn 1:3.   60 Jn 17:3.

come and see

MONDAY, BEING LED BY THE SPIRIT OF JESUS

"Again the next day after John stood, and two of his disciples; And looking upon Jesus as he walked, he saith, Behold the Lamb of God! And the two disciples heard him speak, and they followed Jesus. Then Jesus turned, and saw them following, and saith unto them, What seek ye? They said unto him, Rabbi, (which is to say, being interpreted, Master,) where dwellest thou? He saith unto them, Come and see. They came and saw where he dwelt, and abode with him that day: for it was about the tenth hour."[1]

Moonlight and Faith

Monday is the day of the Moon, which receives its light from the sun, symbol of the Risen Christ. As the moon faithfully reflects the sun, so we receive light from Jesus through faith in Him. As the moon casts the sun's light onto the earth at times of darkness, so, when we walk in the darkness of not knowing, our faith illuminates our path with the light of Jesus. Henry Vaughan reflects poetically on this:

> Wise *Nicodemus* saw such light
> As made him know his God by night.
> Most blessed believer he!

1 Jn 1:35–39.

Who in that land of darkness and blind eyes
Thy long expected healing wings could see
When thou didst rise. . . [2]

The moon is associated with silver, the sun with gold; St John of the Cross compared the teachings of faith with silver plating over gold, the latter symbolizing the truth of God in itself. Monday is also the day of the Holy Spirit, through whom we follow Jesus in faith. This is celebrated particularly in the Greek Orthodox Church, but within living memory the day after Pentecost ("Whit Monday") was a national holiday in the United Kingdom — a continuation of the celebration of the gift of the Spirit. Now in the Catholic Church it is the memorial of Our Lady, the Mother of the Church. As the moon reflects the light of the sun, so Mary reflects the light of Christ made known to us through the Church.

Monday is a day for allowing the Spirit to bring to our minds the truths we received through Sunday's deep contemplation of the Lord, for He promised, "The Comforter, which is the Holy Ghost, whom the Father will send in my name, he shall teach you all things, and bring all things to your remembrance, whatsoever I have said unto you."[3] Monday is a day for a new beginning, for being receptive to what Providence shows us, for letting the Spirit draw us closer to the wisdom of the Lord. It invites us to be receptive to the Holy Spirit as Mary was, enabling a new creation. If Saturday is the old man of the week and Sunday the sleeping infant, then Monday is its child. Its special gift is openness.[4] It reminds us that, "Whosoever shall not receive the kingdom of God as a little child, he shall not enter therein."[5] The Lord refers to his disciples as "little ones"[6] and it is when they have a child-like willingness to be shown His way that they are most truly such.

---

2 "The Night" in *The Metaphysical Poets,* intro. and ed. Helen Gardner (London: Penguin, 1971), 280.   3 Jn 14:26.

4 Reflections on the days of the week are indebted to Wolfgang Held, *Rhythms of the Week* (Edinburgh: Floris Books, 2001).   5 Mk 10: 15.

6 For example: Mt 10:42, 18:6.

Where Dwellest Thou?

Such learning of His way is chronicled in St John's gospel. Two of John the Baptist's disciples hear him say of Jesus, "Behold the lamb of God." [7] One of the disciples is Andrew; the other is unnamed but may well be intended to be identified as John, the author of the gospel.[8] He is not named here just as he is not named when he and Peter see the empty tomb, but simply described as "the other disciple, whom Jesus loved."[9] That not naming is not simply the reticent modesty of the author. It is his love that wants to include us in his adventure of discipleship and his being loved by the Lord; it is the love of Christ that wants us too to follow Him and be gathered into that boundless love becoming in our turn beloved disciples. Implicitly inviting us the readers to do likewise, the two disciples follow Him.

> Then Jesus turned, and saw them following, and saith unto them, What seek ye? They said unto him, Rabbi, (which is to say, being interpreted, Master,) where dwellest thou?[10]

The Lord interrogates their purpose, inviting a disclosure of their heart's intention. The gospel asks us this question also. It is the same question about which the Rule of St Benedict expects the one responsible for a novice's care to be concerned: whether he truly seeks God.[11] The gospel of John is as it were the novice master of every Christian disciple, asking "What seek ye?" This question anticipates the question of the Risen Lord to Mary Magdalene, "Whom seekest thou?"[12] The two disciples in the gospel show that they are indeed serious seekers, for in response they ask a question to which the whole of the gospel is an answer. In Greek it is ποὺ μένεις (*pou meneis*) which a note

---

7 Jn 1:37.
8 Cf. *The Jerome Biblical Commentary* (London: Chapman, 1968), 415.
9 Jn 20:2.   10 Jn 1:38.   11 Rule, Chapter 58.
12 Jn 20:15.

in the King James Version indicates can be rendered as "Where abidest thou?" as well as "Where dwellest thou?" The range of meanings of the verb is as full as in its final use in the gospel, as explained in the previous chapter. On a superficial reading it is simply a request for an address, but this meaning includes the deeper one of asking about the Lord's eternal habitation and so asking Him about the eternal life to which this gospel so often refers. He answers, "Come and see."

Their response has the directness and simplicity of children ready to learn: "They came and saw where he dwelt, and abode with him that day: for it was the tenth hour."[13] It contains the story of discipleship; it is the fourth gospel in miniature. They, and we also as His disciples, see His dwelling (which is to say His life) and they, and we, share it. This life is abiding and eternal. It is an abiding with Him. "That day" which is shared with Him is the eternal day. It is the day referred to in the psalm which in Christian tradition celebrates the resurrection: "This is the day which the LORD hath made; we will rejoice and be glad in it."[14] It is the fullness of life which Jesus spoke of giving His followers: "I am come that they might have life, and that they might have it more abundantly."[15] The fullness is indicated by "the tenth hour" for ten is all-encompassing, being the sum of one (the divine), two (the duality of the created), three (the spirit) and four (the earth, with its dimensions) and, with its repetition of the numeral one leads all (which of itself is nought, symbolized by that figure) back to the divine unity.[16]

As well as pointing beyond time, the "tenth hour" indicates on the temporal level that it is just two hours short of night. It anticipates the saying of Jesus later in the gospel, "Yet a little while is the light with you. Walk while ye have the light, lest darkness come upon you."[17] The quest for eternal day, begun with the question, "Where dwellest thou?" is urgent. The

---

13 Jn 1:39.   14 Ps 118:24.   15 Jn 10:10.
16 See Wolfgang Held, *The Quality of Numbers 1 to 31* (Edinburgh: Floris Books, 2012).   17 Jn 12:35.

invitation to theophany, "Come and see," echoes through John's gospel. In the first chapter Philip repeats it to Nathanael when the latter, in response to the announcement of the finding of Jesus, questions whether "any good thing" can "come out of Nazareth."[18] In Chapter 4, the Samaritan woman says of Jesus, "Come, see a man, which told me all things that ever I did: is not this the Christ?"[19] In the penultimate chapter John "came first to the sepulchre, and he saw, and believed."[20] The gospel invites us also to come and see, to "taste and see that the LORD is good."[21] It asks us whether we want to abide eternally in the fullness of light or to be lost eternally in the periphery of night, "for he that walketh in darkness knoweth not whither he goeth."[22] It resonates with the meanings of μένειν (*menein*): do we want to abide, tarry, remain, dwell, stay, continue with the Lord Christ?

The Abiding of Jesus

Even before this question is asked the gospel has told us where He abides: "in the bosom (εἰς τὸν κόλπον / *eis ton kolpon*) of the Father."[23] It goes on to invite us to abide there through a similar relationship with Him: leaning "on Jesus' bosom (ἐν τῷ κόλπῳ τοῦ Ἰησοῦ / *en tō kolpō tou Iēsou*),"[24] modeled by the one whose "testimony is true."[25] It tells us the wonders performed by the Lord Jesus so that we may "know and believe" in the intimacy of His relationship with the Father, that He tells the truth when He says, "The Father is in me and I in him."[26] Indeed, although Philip does not know it when he issues this invitation, to "come and see" Jesus is no less than to see the Father, as Philip is later told plainly by Jesus: "He who hath seen me hath seen the Father."[27] The identity is abiding: in the Lord's explanation "The words that I speak unto you I speak not of myself; but

18 Jn 1:45–46.
19 Jn 4:29.
20 Jn 20:8.
21 Ps 34:8.
22 Jn 12:35.
23 Jn 1:18.
24 Jn 13:23.
25 Jn 21:24.
26 Jn 10:38.
27 Jn 14:9–10.

the Father that dwelleth in me, he doeth the works." The word "dwelleth" renders μένων (*menōn*) meaning "abiding" with the full force of the uses of other forms of it.[28] The same verb is used when John the Baptist is told, "Upon whom thou shalt see the Spirit descending, and remaining on him, the same is he which baptizeth with the Holy Spirit."[29] The "remaining" is "abiding": the presence is both enduring and living. Through this and the texts about the Father abiding we are being taught about the eternal abiding in the Trinity of Jesus as God. It is this that we are invited to "come and see" and ultimately to share: the abiding of the Father in Him and the abiding of the Spirit on Him.

And His abiding also: He abides and we are called to share that abiding. In the priesthood of all believers we participate in what is said of Him in the letter to the Hebrews: "This man because he continueth ever, hath an unchangeable priesthood."[30] The verb "continueth" translates μένειν (*menein*): Jesus *abides* forever. He is the Christ of whom it is prophesied, "His name shall be called "Wonderful, Counseller, The mighty God, the everlasting Father, the Prince of Peace."[31] The divine abiding of Jesus includes undying life, but it is also an abiding fidelity: "he abideth faithful: he cannot deny himself."[32] Here St Paul is contrasting His fidelity with a possible lack of faith on our part, echoing the Old Testament repeated chronicling of the steadfast fidelity of God in face of repeated infidelity on the part of Israel and identifying Him with that divine fidelity. As Ezekiel tells us that God in tenderness for Jerusalem says, "I will establish unto thee an everlasting covenant,"[33] so John tells us that Jesus in his fidelity to His disciples "loved them unto the end."[34] He is "the good shepherd" who "giveth his life for the sheep" rather than flee like the "hireling."[35] In sharing His undying life with us through love He invites us to share His fidelity through grace. That is ultimately a fidelity to our heavenly homeland.

---

28 Jn 14:10.   29 Jn 1:33.   30 Heb 7:24.   31 Is 9:6.

32 2 Tm 2:13.   33 Ez 16:60.   34 Jn 13:1.   35 Jn 10:12–13.

No Continuing City

"Here we have no continuing city," says the letter to the Hebrews, "but we seek one to come."[36] The word rendered "continuing" is again a form of μένειν (*menein*): we have here nowhere abiding to live. We are "strangers and pilgrims."[37] Only "that great city, the holy Jerusalem, descending out of heaven from God, Having the glory of God"[38] truly abides. The light of the New Jerusalem is "like unto a stone most precious, even like a jasper stone, clear as crystal."[39] The stone symbolizes the enduring quality of the light. The city does not know the earthly changes of the setting of the sun and the rising of the moon;[40] there is "no night"[41] there for "the Lamb is the light thereof."[42] The city abides in the abiding light of Christ who "abideth for ever."[43] Concomitant with being citizens of this city is being, like our Divine Exemplar, neither earthed nor nested here in this world, for "foxes have holes, and birds of the air have nests; but the Son of man hath not where to lay his head."[44] To be of no fixed abode here on earth would, it seems, to be more liable to vicissitudes, even to be disreputable, yet everything under the changing moon is subject to variation and decay. To invest one's heart "where moth and rust doth corrupt, and where thieves break through and steal"[45] is to walk into heartbreak. Rather, says the Apostle, "Seek those things which are above, where Christ sitteth on the right hand of God. Set your affection on things above, not on things on the earth."[46] The heart so set is "hid with Christ in God"[47] and so steadfast — even steadfastly tender — amongst this world's changes.

Heavenly Abiding

Such a heart is in the world, "not of the world."[48] It moves from one task to another without demanding the right to stay, after the manner of Jesus, "he, and his mother, and his brethren,

36 Heb 13:14.	37 1 Pt 2:11.	38 Rv 21:10–11.	39 Rv 21:11.
40 Rv 21:23.	41 Rv 21:25.	42 Rv 21:23.	43 Jn 12:34.
44 Lk 9:58.	45 Mt 6:19.	46 Col 31–2.	47 Col 3:3.
48 Jn 17:16.			

and his disciples," who "went down to Capernaum" and "continued there not many days."[49] The word rendered "continued" meaning "abode" is a form of μένειν (*menein*) here indicating a lack of earthly abiding, but it is also used in John's gospel to denote an abiding of the heart in heaven while yet on earth. Such abiding as this gives strength in the face of hostility as when the enemies of Jesus "sought again to take him: but he escaped out of their hand, And went away again beyond Jordan into the place where John at first baptized; and there he abode."[50] That is to say: where the Spirit descended "from heaven like a dove, and it abode upon him."[51] He went to the place of abiding; he was steadfast in the Trinity. The same strategy is used as the threat intensifies: "Then from that day forth they took counsel together for to put him to death. Jesus therefore walked no more openly among the Jews; but went thence unto a country near to the wilderness, into a city called Ephraim, and there continued with his disciples."[52] He "continued," that is to say "abided" — again a form of μένειν (*menein*) — with His disciples: a heavenly abiding such as He is instructing them to find. This is in miniature what He did in the forty days and forty nights in the wilderness before His baptism: he retreated to find His strength and peace in the Father abiding within Him and the Spirit abiding upon Him. As He took His disciples then into the wilderness to learn to find this strength and peace, so He does now, inviting them to enter into retreat. This practice, which is of obligation for priests and religious in the Catholic Church and recommended for all, is needed for the heart to become established in its heavenly abiding so that the challenges, changes and confrontations of the world do not sway it.

A retreat like this is a time for realizing where our true peace is to be found: not in arrangements we make to secure our future in this world, but above. Henry Vaughan wrote about this in his poem *Peace*:

49 Jn 2:12.   50 Jn 10:39–40.   51 Jn 1:32.   52 Jn 11:53–54.

> My Soul, there is a Countrie
>   Far beyond the stars,
> Where stands a winged Sentrie
>   All skillfull in the wars,
> There above the noise, and danger
>   Sweet peace sits crown'd with smiles,
> And one born in a Manger
>   Commands the Beauteous files,
> He is thy gracious friend,
>   And (O my soul, awake!)
> Did in pure love descend
>   To die here for thy sake,
> If thou canst get but thither,
>   There growes the flowre of peace,
> The Rose that cannot wither,
>   Thy fortresse, and thy ease;
> Leave then thy foolish ranges;
>   For none can thee secure,
> But one who never changes,
>   Thy God, thy life, thy Cure.[53]

We can get "thither" now through contemplative prayer for that opens us to the eternal. We do not need to wait for the Lord to make Himself known at the final and apocalyptic swallowing up of time by eternity, we can wait on Him now for He wants to be immediately and eternally present to us. The "one who never changes" offers us a peace which our "foolish ranges" in the world cannot give. If you who are reading this book are in retreat right now, stay with it! It will not mean that you never have to deal with trouble, but it will help you to be aware that trouble is not absolute (it does not belong to that realm) and even now you can "cast all your care upon him; for he careth for you."[54]

---

53 *The Metaphysical Poets*, intro. and ed. Helen Gardner (London: Penguin, 1971), 269.   54 1 Pt 5:7.

The most remarkable instance of the Lord Jesus in such a retreat (apart from the forty days in the desert and the Garden of Gethsemane) is immediately after He receives the news of the mortal illness of Lazarus: "Now Jesus loved Martha, and her sister, and Lazarus. When he heard therefore that he was sick, he abode two days still in the same place where he was."[55] If we take "abode" (ἔμεινεν / *emeinen*) simply in the banal sense of "stay" it is impossible to make sense of this: what would "therefore" refer to — "because he loved them"? If so, then delaying to help looks to be the very opposite of what love would urge. If however "abode" refers to abiding in the "place where he was" and that is understood as His indwelling in the Trinity, then it makes perfect sense for that is where He finds the power to give life. In this case "where he was" could mean where He had His being and life, "For as the Father hath life in himself; so hath he given to the Son to have life in himself."[56] This abiding "two days" may also be proleptic of His two days abiding in the tomb whence He rises so that "the dead shall hear the voice of the Son of God: and they that hear shall live."[57] It points in any case to the value of biding one's time, of dwelling in divine life, of contemplation before undertaking action. We are called to abide.

Peter and John

The Church depends on this abiding. It is modeled in Peter and John, in both of whom — as embodying Christian discipleship and membership of the Church — we need to see ourselves. Peter is identified with a stone, which is a natural symbol of the eternal and abiding: the Lord says to him, "Thou shalt be called Cephas, which is by interpretation, A stone."[58] This also identifies him with Christ, the "chief corner stone,"[59] whose vicar he is. He learns from bitter experience that his staying power is not his own, but comes from reliance on God: as the Lord predicts he betrays Him

---

55 Jn 11:5-6.   56 Jn 5:26.   57 Jn 5:25.
58 Jn 1:42.   59 1 Pt 2:6.

three times before the cock crows, but his destiny is to "glorify God" by his death.[60] As a stone manifests eternity in this world, so Peter proclaims the undying "word of God which liveth and abideth for ever,"[61] concerning the message of which the Lord said, "Heaven and earth shall pass away: but my words shall not pass away."[62] His teaching of God's word is the stone in the herbaceous garden — "The grass withereth, and the flower thereof falleth away: But the word of the Lord endureth for ever."[63] He lives on in the popes who succeed him: they proclaim the abiding truth of God *Urbi et Orbi* — to the city and to the world. Peter is established in what is eternal as a rock, giving stable leadership to the Lord's followers in this proclamation, but it is John whose special vocation is simply to abide in eternity like his loving and beloved Lord. Peter promulgates the abiding, John receives and rests in what abides. Peter shows the eternal to this world; John beholds the eternal in the next. The emphasis is: Peter loves; John is loved. Loving the Lord is what equips the Christian to care for others — that is why the Lord asks Peter about this three times[64] — but it is "the disciple whom Jesus loved"[65] who models a Christian's essential identity. Love for the Lord begins with His love of us. St Teresa of Ávila pointed to the heart of Christian life when she spoke of "taking time frequently to be alone with him who we know loves us."[66] That knowing we are loved is the beginning of everything and the reason that retreats — frequent short retreats and regular longer ones — matter so much. The Christian disciple can and should sometimes take a break from the Petrine-style active proclamation of Christian truth, but his or her believing heart needs always to know the Lord's love.

To do that, we need to be in relationship with Him. John models that for us. Here is a key account: "Now there was

60　Jn 13:38; 18:17, 25–27; 21:19.　　　61　1 Pt 1:23.　　　62　Mk 13:31.

63　1 Pt 1:24–25.　　　64　Cf Jn 21:15–19.　　　65　Jn 21:20.

66　*The Book of Her Life* 8,5 in *The Collected Works of St Teresa of Ávila*, trans. K. Kavanaugh O.C.D. and O. Rodriguez O.C.D. (Washington, DC: ICS Institute of Carmelite Studies, 1976), 1, 67.

leaning on Jesus' bosom one of his disciples, whom Jesus loved. Simon Peter therefore beckoned to him, that he should ask who it should be of whom he spake. He then lying on Jesus' breast saith unto him, Lord, who is it? Jesus answered, He it is, to whom I shall give a sop, when I have dipped it."[67] It is the intimacy of this that is striking. We might expect John to unfold the secret of his life to the Lord, but it is more surprising that John can ask what is in the heart of Jesus. Yet there is no reason to suppose Him to be less generous in self-disclosure than His followers. Indeed, He has said, "Henceforth I call you not servants; for the servant knoweth not what his lord doeth: but I have called you friends; for all things that I have heard of my Father I have made known to you."[68] The last clause is remarkable, since the Son speaks everything that the Father has to say. He is the Father's only Word. Even the entire creation made through Him does not exhaust what is expressed through Him. John, the beloved disciple, has privileged access to this. Why? One can only speculate, but my intuition is that it is because he has allowed himself to be loved. To come to the Lord Jesus with openness and trust, willing to receive all that He wants to give, is to know more than all the secrets of the universe. This is not a question of being well-endowed with gifts such as intelligence: the teaching that the Lord gave about the widow's "two mites which make a farthing" applies to understanding as much as to riches.[69] Giving all, however little, we receive all. If we open our hearts with whatever is in them to the Lord, He opens to us His own heart, human in its sympathy and divine in its depth. Such an encounter is unburdening: in it, we confidently cast all our care on Him, for He cares for us.[70] It is a leaning on Jesus, as John leans on him. It is finding support where it truly is and not where it only appears to be to the eyes of the addicted psyche. No substance, no comfort, no prop in the world can give what He gives. We can bring Him any and

67 Jn 13:23–26.   68 Jn 15:15.   69 Mk 12:42.   70 Cf 1 Pt 5:7.

every concern, whether our own or another's. That is best done without pressing specific answers on Him but rather entrusting Him with complete liberty of action on our behalf. It is more a matter of being there for a heart to heart than telling Him the things we want Him to do. And if He has a specific answer, we will know it by an intuition of the heart and by events and the opportunities they present.

In all of this John is our exemplar, but it is important to note that Scripture bears witness that John acted with Peter. To Peter also "it is given to know the mystery of the kingdom of God."[71] John is the contemplative in particular, Peter is (because of his leadership) in a special sense every Christian. To be, as John was, with Peter is to be in fellowship and communion with the whole of the Church led by Peter. This is a life-giving fellowship and communion embodied in the successor of Peter, the Pope. Together we are led to pray, as the Lord "took Peter and John and James, and went up into a mountain to pray";[72] together we witness the transfiguration of the Lord as "Jesus taketh Peter, James, and John his brother, and bringeth them up into a high mountain apart, And was transfigured before them";[73] together we accompany Him in the garden where "he took with him Peter and the two sons of Zebedee"[74] and together we gather at the empty tomb as "Peter therefore went forth, and that other disciple, and came to the sepulchre."[75] Our witness to the resurrection is reciprocal, as "that disciple whom Jesus loved saith unto Peter, It is the Lord"[76] and Peter proclaimed, "This Jesus hath God raised up, whereof we are all witnesses."[77] As "Peter and John went up together into the temple at the hour of prayer"[78] so together we celebrate the liturgy; together we perform acts of mercy, as they responded to the lame man when "Peter, fastening his eyes upon him with John, said, Look on

---

71 Mk 4:11, Cf. Jean Borella, *Christ the Original Mystery: Esoterism & the Mystical Way* (Brooklyn: Angelico Press, 2018), 283, footnote 3.

72 Lk 9:28.   73 Mt 17:1–2.   74 Mt 26:37.

75 Jn 20:3.   76 Jn 21:7.   77 Acts 2:32.   78 Acts 3:1.

us";[79] together, in the Spirit, we share "the boldness of Peter and John."[80] Together we invoke the Holy Spirit as Peter and John, sent among the Samaritans, "prayed for them, that they might receive the Holy Ghost."[81]

The Holy Spirit

It is the Holy Spirit who unites us to Peter and John, and indeed to the whole Church. The Holy Spirit brings about the Church, gathers its members into one living body, is the soul of the Church. Monday, the day of the Holy Spirit, is the day to remember this. The contemporary tendency is to think of our belonging to each other as something negotiated by independent individuals. Yet it is not like that at all. We do not come on the scene as fully formed human actors. We enter as Monday's creatures, little children. We do not have words; we receive them from other people. We do not have food; we receive it from others. We little by little learn to take part in a conversation that began long before we were there, like people turning up late at a party when most people have gone and those left have started washing the glasses. We can only contribute what we are given and if we are thanked for it that is in the spirit of courtesy of a hostess who thanks her guest for handing her the plate on which are the cheese straws she made herself. We do not have a history; we receive it from those who are older than us. It is impossible for a separated individual even to survive for long, let alone flourish, in the days following birth. The autonomous individual may be the focus of much mental consideration, but he or she is not the abiding reality. That is the Holy Spirit, that is to say God, who makes us one, "For by one Spirit are we all baptized into one body, whether we be Jews or Gentiles, whether we be bond or free; and have been all made to drink into one Spirit."[82] There is a real sense, therefore, in which in the Holy Spirit we are each other. So in reflecting on how Peter and John model

79 Acts 3:4.   80 Acts 4:13.   81 Acts 8:15.   82 1 Cor 12:13.

different aspects of Christian discipleship, both of which need to be part of our walk with the Lord, we are Peter, we are John. That is the abiding reality. That is love, which is God. We each have our particularities and foibles, yet these are not our deepest and abiding truth: that is what is beyond everything passing, and shared with all. Our deepest and abiding truth is simply God. This is to say that it is love that lasts, not selfishness. When we love our neighbor as our self we realize our abiding identity.

The seventh-century monk and theologian St Maximus the Confessor identifies this realization as the summit of interior liberty, that is to say, the possession of perfect charity. One who has reached it no longer differentiates between self and other, slave and free, man and woman. Having got out of the zone where passions reign, he only sees in men and women their one nature. He sees all as being on the same level; he has the same heart for all. "There is neither Jew nor Greek, there is neither bond nor free, there is neither male nor female: for ye are all one in Christ Jesus."[83]

This perfect charity is not usually there when we first set off on our spiritual quest, when we, with the two disciples, ask the Lord, "Where abidest thou?" We walk with Him towards the place where the Spirit of love abides; we enter by steps into the Spirit of truth. Of course we could not do that if the Spirit had not first come into our history with "a sound from heaven as of a mighty rushing wind" and the sight of "cloven tongues like as of fire."[84] We could not have the intuition of love in which we communicate with the essence of others if those before us had not first spoken "as the Spirit gave them utterance" and had not "every man heard them speak in his own language."[85] We could not find the Spirit if the Spirit had not first found us in founding the Church to manifest His truth and gather us into love. We simply need "to

---

83 *Sources Chrétiennes: Centuries sur la Charité* (Paris: Éditions du Cerf, 1943), 2.30, 103; Gal 3:28.
84 Acts 2:2–3.   85 Acts 2:4–6.

be converted, and become as little children."[86] A little child can learn anyone's language; indeed one whose parents speak different native tongues normally learns both. To become a child again on the way into the kingdom of heaven is not literally to become a linguist. It is rather to receive the Spirit who is the essence of the meaning of everyone's word-world. It is to know in the depths of our being the depths of everyone's being. It is simply realization, in the double sense of becoming aware of a presence and of making actual a potential. The awareness of the presence, of the Spirit leading us to know "that Jesus is the Lord"[87] brings us to know that "Christ is all, and in all"[88] so that in Him "there is neither Greek nor Jew,"[89] neither, essentially, friend nor foe and neither mine and yours, for in truth and love we belong together and to each other. God the Holy Spirit gathers us together in communion and community so that we actualize in word and deed our oneness in Christ, in whom we abide. The next chapter speaks of what that abiding is and how it is reached.

---

86 Mt 18:3.

87 1 Cor 12:3.   88 Col 3:11   89 1 Thes 3:11.

abide in me

TUESDAY, THE STRUGGLE TO LOVE

> *"Abide in me, and I in you. As the branch cannot*
> *bear fruit of itself, except it abide in the vine,*
> *no more can ye, except ye abide in me. I am*
> *the vine, ye are the branches: He that abideth in*
> *me, and I in him, the same bringeth forth much*
> *fruit: for without me ye can do nothing."*[1]

Mars

There is an ancient association between being a Christian and
being a soldier. It finds expression in the hymn "Onward Christian soldiers." It is at its most stark in the writing of Saint Paul:

> Put on the whole armour of God, that ye may be able
> to stand against the wiles of the devil. For we wrestle
> not against flesh and blood, but against principalities,
> against powers, against the rulers of the darkness
> of this world, against spiritual wickedness in high
> places. Wherefore take unto you the whole armour of
> God, that ye may be able to withstand in the evil day,
> and having done all, to stand. Stand therefore, having your loins girt about with truth, and having on
> the breastplate of righteousness; and your feet shod
> with the preparation of the gospel of peace; Above
> all taking the shield of faith, wherewith ye shall be
> able to quench all the fiery darts of the wicked. And

---

1 Jn 15:4–5.

take the helmet of salvation and the sword of the
Spirit, which is the word of God.[2]

The word "stand" echoes through this passage. The Apostle
exhorts us to stand firm, to abide in the Lord. Abiding is a martial business. Tuesday is the day of Mars, god of war (as in the
French *mardi*) and so linked to the martial. The English name
for the day comes from the Old English *tiwesdæg*, from *Tiwes*,
genitive of *Tiw*, and *dæg*, meaning "day." This is a translation of
the Latin *dies Martis*, the day of Mars.[3] Tiw (his Anglo-Saxon
name) or Tyr (his Old Norse name) was identified with the
Roman god Mars. In Norse mythology he is a war god, but also
the god who, more than any other, presides over matters of law
and justice.[4] In the myth *The Binding of Fenrir* Tyr makes a
heroic sacrifice for the sake of law and justice. When the gods
see that the dreadful wolf, Fenrir, will soon no longer be a
puppy they fear for their lives, so they try to bind him with
a dwarf-fashioned chain from which he cannot escape. This is
curiously light for it is fashioned from things not of this world:
"the sound of a cat's footfall and the woman's beard, the mountain's roots and the bear's sinews and the fish's breath and bird's
spittle." When he sees it, Fenrir is suspicious, and will only allow
the gods to put the chain around him if one of them will stick a
hand in his mouth as a pledge of good faith. Only Tyr is willing
to do so. When the wolf finds himself unable to break free, he
bites off Tyr's hand.[5] Tuesday, his day, is therefore a day for making sacrifices in the battle for what is right and just. There is an
ancient connection between battle and justice, with a duel being
used as legal process to establish the right of a claimant. For

2 Eph 6:11–17.
3 https://www.etymonline.com/word/Tuesday#etymonline_v_18795
4 https://norse-mythology.org/gods-and-creatures/the-aesir-gods-and
-goddesses/tyr/
5 Snorri Sturluson, *Edda*, trans. and ed. by Anthony Faulkes (London: J.M.
Dent Everyman, 1995), 28–29.

example, in the works of the chronicler of King Arthur, Thomas Malory, one knight will say to another with whom he is in contention that he will prove the truth of his claim upon the body of the other. Such valor belongs to Tuesday. If Monday is the day for being open and receptive, for seeing what we are called to, then Tuesday is the day for taking a stand, in readiness to confront whatever would shake our resolve to abide.

That is not simply about confronting the powers of darkness, as in the passage above from Saint Paul. It is also about confronting our weaknesses, fighting to conquer passions that would thwart the Spirit of love. The battle front for this varies from person to person. War is undertaken with hostile, not friendly, powers and we have different enemies within. It would therefore be presumptuous and wrong of me to tell you where to concentrate your forces, but I would say this: virtue is won in battle. So it is the sex-crazed person who wins through to being chaste and the one given to hardly controllable fits of rage who is victoriously patient. No one is called a fighter for knocking down a weakling. Love for the Lord is proven in battle and we should thank God for our weaknesses because they give us the opportunity to do something beautiful for Him. The merely inert do not have this opportunity for holiness: there is less room for them to grow in strength of virtue. That is not quite true, however: God in His providence does not leave anyone without opportunity. There is always the possibility of doing battle with one's inertia! We are all invited to have "heroic hearts," to be "strong in will" and "not to yield."[6] Armed with truth, righteousness, and faith, we are to fight to be constant in our abiding in the Lord Jesus.

The Vine

To step out in faith like this, we need our "feet shod with the preparation of the gospel of peace."[7] We need to look to the gospel to see, in order that it may be the better defended, how we

6 Tennyson, "Ulysses."   7 Eph 6:15.

can picture this abiding. When Jesus says, "I am the vine, ye are the branches"[8] He gives us a symbol full of implications. A vine can be very old, with thick gnarled branches; at the same time it bears fresh grapes, young and vital. Such is God: ever ancient, ever new; venerable and vital. The grapes suggest the Eucharist and so the cup of suffering Jesus is given to drink. When Peter tries to tell Him not to drink of it, He rebukes him[9] and goes on to say to His disciples that they too need to partake of it: "If any man will come after me, let him deny himself, and take up his cross, and follow me."[10] To be part of this vine is to share the passion of Christ who asks, "Can ye drink of the cup that I drink of?"[11] Not to be part of it is to be "cast forth as a branch" and burned in the fire.[12] That is a loss of true life, which is only to be found in abiding in the vine from which the grapes are to be crushed, for the Lord tells us, "Whosoever will save his life shall lose it; and whosoever will lose his life for my sake shall find it."[13] We are called to "abide (μένη / mene) in the vine,"[14] which is to say our vocation is to dwell, stay, continue, remain in Him who says, "Abide in me."[15] What is this abiding and how do we come to it? First, let us consider what it is.

What is it to abide in the Lord?

It is more real than dwelling in something physical, such as a house. As eternity transcends time and is more real, so this abiding transcends space and is more real. It is metaphysical. Since "God is a Spirit"[16] and as such not extended in space and time and since He gives life to the soul, to dwell or abide in Him is to share the life of all and to be present in everything as He is present in everything. Although this abiding transcends space, we can use the spatial as a metaphor and say that in our inmost being, where God is, we can share His universal presence. That inward abiding unites us with all that is out there: an interior

8 Jn 15:5.   9 Mt 16:22–23.   10 Mt 16:24.   11 Mk 10:38.
12 Jn 15:6.   13 Mt 16:25.   14 Jn 15:4.   15 Jn 15:4.
16 Jn 4:24.

life with God within gives us a harmonious relationship with what is outward. To acknowledge God's transcendence as well as His immanence we also need to say that God is beyond all that is out there. This abiding in the Lord is altogether more real than being in a particular space and time, for these pass away and He does not. Yet it has its particularity, an absolute and eternal particularity, in the person of Christ. That particularity includes every particularity, for "all things were made by him."[17] Its reality belongs to the traditional artistic perspective discussed in Chapter 1: not the perspective of a single fixed point in time and space, but the perspective of many eyes. St John the Divine has a vision of such: "In the midst of the throne, and round about the throne, were four beasts full of eyes, before and behind."[18] The throne is "set in heaven"[19] and the beasts are "full of eyes within."[20] Together they image the all-seeing omniscience of the Omnipotent. Abiding in the Lord, therefore, does not exclude; it touches all who are, in the very depth of their being where God sustains and gives life to them. Although as embodied people we exclude one person by paying attention to another on the physical level, through abiding in the Lord we include all in loving attention spiritually, for no one is neglected in God. Miracles of bilocation (which manifest this spiritual reality to the eyes of others) may be rare, but souls who attain to some sort of universal love in Christ are more commonly met.

This love, because of its divine depth, can love people better than they love themselves, not with an officiousness that thinks it knows what is best for them but with an intuition whose source is the very essence of their life and value: God's gaze upon them. And people know when they are loved. From this comes the sense that ordinary unpretentious folk have that the saints are on their side, sinners though they be. This can be manifest in all sorts of situations. A religious sister told me that once she was waiting on a platform in the Paris Metro. On the

17 Jn 1:3.   18 Rv 4:6.   19 Rv 4:2.   20 Rv 4:8.

platform across the track lay a drunken man. He called out, "Sainte Thérèse! Sainte Thérèse!" He was not sober enough to realize that this sister belonged to a different order from St Thérèse, nor that the saint was not around to take the metro, but he did realize (it seems to me) that St Thérèse loved him. Being loved like this, with the love of Christ, helps people let go of a drivenness that compels them to anxious concern about (for example) their looks, their financial resources or their academic achievement. A craving for the (less than complete) love that they may have experienced or seen given to others on account of such things can be dropped as they relax into the all-enveloping love that comes from God and through His friends. This universal love makes sense of consecrated celibacy and anticipates resurrection life in which "they neither marry, nor are given in marriage."[21] It transcends the limitations of this world. Space and time are not absolute; God is. That truth is reflected mathematically in Bell's theorem, which demonstrates that reality is non-local, and in the findings of quantum physics in which particles influence each other from afar. This abiding reality makes sense of Lazarus in the parable being "carried by the angels into Abraham's bosom,"[22] which on the literal level sounds strange yet spiritually understood expresses the sharing of the life enjoyed by the saints in heaven. "In Christ" or "in Our Lady" is not a pious fiction: it is real. In Spirit we are one, hence the third Eucharistic Prayer of the Mass asks "that we, who are nourished by the Body and Blood of your Son and filled with his Holy Spirit, may become one body, one spirit in Christ."

Reflecting metaphysically can offer an understanding of this. "Existence" is in common parlance taken to refer to the whole of life, but in truth we can live without existing: we can live in the source of our being, in God. That is our truest life. The following reflections by a Catholic thinker of the last century clarify this:

21 Mt 22:30.   22 Lk 16:22.

All creatures are one without confusion, it is understood, in their principial non-existence. For the oneness where all name is gone is not a state of existence: not at least in the precise and only really useful sense of existence — standing out. It is not a standing out, it is a standing in. In the oneness where all name is gone there is no real distinction: no real, only virtual, distinction of the creature from God.[23]

"The oneness where all name is gone" (the phrase is from Meister Eckhart) is the place (to speak metaphorically) of communion. Words like "principial" and "virtual" in the above citation denoting life in this oneness make it sound as though it is not at all substantial — maybe ghostly or even imaginary — but that is because we mistake existence for abiding reality. From the perspective of existence there is in this "truest life" only a potential life; from an eternal perspective it is the only fully real life. Here, in the words of John Donne's prayer, there is "no darkness nor dazzling, but one equal light; no noise nor silence, but one equal music; no fears nor hopes, but one equal possession; no ends nor beginnings, but one equal eternity."[24] Here God is our life and since He is the life of all others also we are one with them. That does not abolish our or their personhood, any more than it abolishes the persons of the Holy Trinity. It simply gives unity. Divine life keeps us in existence, but it is an "undiscovered country" for the most part while we are on the earth, because we are habituated to pay attention to the outward and existent aspect of our life. This is not to say that there is never any awareness of it: sometimes it is uncovered, and not just through apparitions of Our Lady and the saints. To take an example from another tradition, the thirteenth-century Persian mystical poet Rumi suffered the disappearance of his friend

23 *A Catholic Mind Awake: The Writings of Bernard Kelly*, ed. and intro. by Scott Randall Paine (Brooklyn: Angelico Press, 2017), 69.
24 https://www.stmw.org/donne.html

Shams of Tabriz with whom he had an intense spiritual bond. He journeyed to search for him and came to the realization:

> Why should I seek? I am the same as he. His essence speaks through me. I have been looking for myself![25]

In other words, he came to know his true life which was none other than the true life of his beloved friend. It is as though east and west met at the North Pole.

We live that abiding, united, spiritual life by being concerned with what is seen by eyes "round about the throne"[26] rather than our own, with God's all-seeing rather than our limited perspective, with the invisible rather than the visible "for the things which are seen are temporal; but the things which are unseen are eternal."[27] In this life of the Spirit there is universal connection, something which modern information technology imitates on a lower plane without offering the same joy of communion. Indeed, in this context the traditional prayer to the Holy Spirit is, perhaps unconsciously, mined for a brand name.[28] The abiding reality of this life is unshakeable: it does not suffer from the relative weakness of solid bodies, which, as Plotinus pointed out, are vulnerable to exclusion by each other.[29] That which includes the other in Christ cannot be excluded by the other. What is true and abiding does not have the frailty even of what appears strongest on the earth, as Emily Dickinson realizes in this poem:

> The Truth — is stirless —
> Other force — may be presumed to move —

25 "On Rumi," in *Rumi Selected Poems*, trans. by Coleman Banks with John Mayne, A.J. Arberry and Reynold Nicholson (London: Penguin, 1995), xii.
26 Rv 4:6.   27 2 Cor 4:18.
28 "... en*kindle* in them the fire of your love"
29 Robert Bolton, *The Keys of Gnosis* (Hillsdale NY: Sophia Perennis, 2004), 66, quoting *Enneads* 3,6,6.

This — then — is best for confidence —
When oldest Cedars swerve —

And Oaks untwist their fists —
And Mountains — feeble — lean —
How excellent a Body, that
Stands without a Bone

How vigorous a Force
That holds without a Prop — Truth stays
Herself — and every man
That trusts Her — boldly up — [30]

The Bible identifies truth with God: His Spirit is stronger than "other force" that "may be presumed to move," a presumption that ignores its being held eternally still in the divine perspective and design.

This abiding in truth gives freedom, confidence and joy. The Lord says, "If ye continue in my word, then are ye my disciples indeed; And ye shall know the truth and the truth shall make you free."[31] His word opens up for us the unseen and greater reality and indicates what actions conform to this reality, enabling us to find our life in it. If we abide in His word ("continue" renders μείνητε / *meinēte*, the same word that is translated elsewhere as "abide") we are set free: because it liberates us from the distortions of selfishness into truth, because it unlinks us from partiality to ground us in the essence of all that is, because if we abide in this reality we have essentially nothing to lose. We are made free from anxiety about losing particular things. In such an abiding we can be confident of an unlimited accomplishment. The Lord promises us: "If ye abide in me, and my words abide in you, ye shall ask what ye will, and it shall be done for you."[32] This is because in such an abiding we will what

30 https://www.poemhunter.com/poem/the-truth-is-stirless/
31 Jn 8:31–32.   32 Jn 15:7.

He wills: we do not "ask amiss" for the sake of private "lusts,"[33] for His Spirit inspires us to seek what leads to true happiness for ourselves and for others. John in his first letter urges us to abide in Him so that we may have confidence even in the blaze of truth of the second coming: "Abide in him; that, when he shall appear, we may have confidence, and not be ashamed before him at his coming."[34] Since "whosoever abideth in him, sinneth not"[35] there is good reason for such confidence. The abiding accounts too for the confident "boldness of Peter and John"[36] and the apostles speaking "the word of God with boldness."[37]

Ultimately we are given His teaching about abiding in Him for the sake of our joy. The Lord explains: "These things I have spoken unto you, that my joy might remain in you, and that your joy might be full."[38] The abiding joy is, He indicates, for others also: "I have chosen you, and ordained you, that ye should go and bring forth fruit, and that your fruit should remain."[39] The fruit that remains or abides (μένῃ / *menē*) is the joy of others who also have the freedom, scope for action, confidence of abiding. That joy becomes ours also, an eternal joy.

How to Abide in the Lord

Such is our abiding in the Lord: being in harmony with all that is; transcending all that is; a free, confident, joyful life of unshakeable steadfastness. How do we get there? First of all, by prayer. Liturgical prayer, the prayer of the Church, has itself an abiding quality. It doesn't finish; it just goes on. Even the end of the liturgical year blends seamlessly with the beginning of the new liturgical year. The fact that the various offices of the day are celebrated at about the same times each day fixes those times so what is celebrated becomes abiding. Every morning is an abiding praise of God because lauds is celebrated every morning; every evening is a continuing rejoicing in God our Savior

33 Jas 4:3.   34 1 Jn 2:28.   35 1 Jn 3:6.   36 Acts 4:13.
37 Acts 4:31.   38 Jn 15:11.   39 Jn 15:16.

since Mary's canticle of praise, which does this, is recited every evening in vespers; every night is an abiding commendation of our spirit into the hands of the Lord since the responsary that does this is sung every night in compline. These acts of worship become abiding because they are performed daily and so each day becomes the eternal day the Lord made in which we rejoice and are glad.[40] Of course not everybody can participate in the liturgy like this, but as already indicated in Chapter 1, simply to come to Mass every Sunday is to participate in this eternal day.

It is not only the daily and the weekly patterns of worship that help us to abide in what does not pass: it is also the yearly cycle of praise. This is so above all because it is patterned after Christ's life, so that it leads us to abide in the One who abides. His birth, His showing to the nations (the Epiphany), His baptism, His transfiguration, His entry into Jerusalem, His death, His resurrection, His ascension into heaven are all marked liturgically so that the year becomes His life and the repetition of the year's liturgy brings us into that abiding life.[41]

A sense of how this happens is given by Thornton Wilder's play, *The Long Christmas Dinner*. It presents ninety years of the history of a family by enacting only their gathering for Christmas dinner, each year in unbroken continuity with the next and characters only leaving the stage when they die and only entering when they are born. The liturgy is something like this. When Christmas comes, it is eternally present even though somebody attending the celebration may be there one year and not the next (or vice-versa). The ever-present quality of the cycle of the liturgy is a stepping out of time. Liturgy is essentially about stepping out of time to be present to eternity and in particular to the One who is eternal, Jesus Christ.

As well as participating in liturgy we can more simply and directly ask Him for mutual indwelling by making a prayer of

40 Cf Ps 118:24.
41 There is more about how the liturgy helps us enter into the eternal in Chapter 6 of my book *The Meaning of Blue*.

His words "Abide in me, and I in you."[42] This can be by way of a repeated prayer phrase to which one returns in times of silent prayer every time one becomes aware that the attention of the heart is wandering. The prayer for abiding doesn't need to be this explicit: the purpose of moving the heart to abide in the Lord will also be served by other short prayers, such as the Jesus prayer: "Lord Jesus Christ, Son of the living God, have mercy on me, a sinner!" Meditation on the life of Christ in the mysteries of the rosary too draws us into His abiding life, as does meditation on that life through the prayerful reading of the gospels. Meditation and prayer as such are an abiding in the Abiding. A continuing in them is an abiding abiding in the Abiding.

When the prayer becomes wordless it takes us beyond time and space, for this sort of prayer is an abiding beyond words and concepts. These latter tie us to this world for they are fashioned from our experience of it and directed to operating in it. Words ("the carnal vesture of meaning")[43] have a certain materiality even when only thought: there is evidence of this in the development of a brain/computer interface where commands given merely mentally can be picked up by technology. Nothing, says Meister Eckhart, is so like God as silence, and the book of Revelation speaks of "silence in heaven."[44] Hence the spiritual quest has to do with silence. This has always been an aspect of cloistered life, as when St Benedict says silence has such a weight of importance that license to speak (albeit about good and holy things) should be allowed rarely, even to perfect disciples.[45] St John of the Cross says, "It is great wisdom to know how to be silent and to look at neither the remarks, nor the deeds, nor the lives of others."[46] These spiritual masters are guiding us away from an eagerness to impose our judgments on others and towards an interior silence where the devices and desires of

42 Jn 15:4.
43 Jean Borella, *Christ the Original Mystery* (Brooklyn: Angelico Press, 2018), 400.   44 Rv 8:1.   45 Chapter 6 of this book.
46 Maxims on Love No 30, *Collected Works of St. John of the Cross*, 676.

our own hearts cease their clamor, so that we can be attentive
to the divine will and desire of God which is infinitely better at
making us happy. Silent prayer is a paying attention to His presence which is ultimately beyond any particular form, for it is the
source of every form. Yet in that silence our hearts can receive
gentle promptings, known as such by the peace that comes with
them and by their abiding over time, which are for our abiding
good for they lead us by good actions to our heavenly homeland.
These promptings are also for the good of others, for no one
ever goes there alone. Prayer is our orientation for the journey.

The essence of prayer is trust. It is as though we are crossing
the murky waters of a river in which there are stepping stones
that do not protrude and cannot be seen. To put a foot down on
one we have to trust that it is there. Similarly we need to trust
in the presence of Christ our rock so that we can walk towards
the Beyond, crossing the river Jordan that separates us from the
Promised Land. If we believe that the solid stone is there we can
step out; if we believe in the abiding presence of Christ we can
be supported by Him as we pass through the troubles of this life
to our eternal destiny. Prayer implies that trust or belief. Hence
it is said *lex orandi lex credendi* — the law of praying is the law of
believing. Belief is formulated from the practice of prayer. And
belief leads to the abiding presence of God: "Whosoever shall
confess that Jesus is the Son of God, God dwelleth in him, and
he in God."[47] "Dwelleth" renders μένει (*menei*), a form of μένειν
(*menein*), the word we have been focusing on. The dwelling or
abiding in Jesus comes from faith in Him: the trust that He is
indeed the Son of God and is a steadfast rock to support us as
we walk through the murky waters of our life here below. Faith
that He truly and eternally abides as God is the ground of our
prayer. Indeed, steadfast belief in what has been revealed to us
through Him is an indicator of the divine indwelling: "He that
abideth in the doctrine of Christ, he hath both the Father and

47 1 Jn 4:15.

the Son."[48] This belief, concomitant of prayer and evidence of divine presence, can be summed up simply in the prayer that St Faustina made known: "Jesus, I trust in you."

Yet "faith without works is dead,"[49] so a living faith born of prayer leads to action. This wholeness of faith with works is required for us to dwell in the Lord. There is no ambiguity about the action linked to faith and abiding in Him. The Scripture is clear: "This is his commandment, that we should believe on the name of his Son, Jesus Christ, and love one another as he gave commandment. And he that keepeth his commandment dwelleth in him, and he in him."[50] The giving of the commandment is explicitly recorded. It immediately follows the passage cited above about joy being the purpose of the Lord's teaching concerning abiding. It indicates the full extent of what is asked: "This is my commandment, that ye love one another as I have loved you. Greater love hath no man than this, that a man lay down his life for his friends."[51] At the least this involves laying down the life of the false ego, the life we must lose to find abiding life in the Lord. Self-importance has to go, for "Charity vaunteth not itself, is not puffed up."[52] Ultimately the invitation is to sacrifice, to offer one's life as Christ Himself offered His, to be grapes on the vine that are taken and crushed to make wine to drink "new in the kingdom of God."[53] The call to mutual love is so central that according to tradition St John in his old age on the island of Patmos condensed all of his profound spiritual teaching into the ever repeated simple injunction: "little children, love one another," recapitulating what he had written earlier: "This is the message that ye heard from the beginning that we should love one another."[54] Abiding in Jesus ineluctably involves loving one another, for to be in the place where He is (the Trinity) is to be united with each other, for it is the place of universal love: "God is love."[55] It is the place in which He prays that we shall (united)

---

48 2 Jn 1:9.   49 Jas 2:20.   50 1 Jn 3:23–24.   51 Jn 15:12–13.
52 1 Cor 13:4.   53 Mk 14:25.   54 1 Jn 3:11.   55 1 Jn 4:8.

abide, asking: "That they all may be one; as thou, Father, art in me, and I in thee, that they also may be one in us."[56] It is impossible to have that loving union with God in the absence of fraternal love: "If a man say, I love God, and hateth his brother, he is a liar."[57] The tender mercy of God towards us cannot be abstracted from our tenderness towards others. Saint Paul makes the point: "And be ye kind to one another, tender hearted, forgiving one another, even as God for Christ's sake hath forgiven you."[58]

So how do we do it? How do we remain tender-hearted? Essentially it is a matter of remaining open to Christ, for that is to be open to all since "without him was not any thing made that was made."[59] We can begin anywhere. It is not even necessary to start with a religious impulse. Any positive regard for another opens the heart, so makes a space for Christ, so a space for all. The fable Grushenka tells in Dostoevsky's *The Karamazov Brothers* is apposite. A wicked woman had been thrown by devils into a burning lake:

> Her guardian angel was looking on and thought to himself: "What good deed can I possibly recall to tell God about?" He remembered one, and said to God: "She once," he said, "picked a spring onion from her garden and gave it to a beggar woman." And God answered him: "Why don't you," he said, "take this same onion, hold it out to her in the lake, and let her grab it and hold tight, and if you manage to pull her out of the lake, may she go to heaven, but if the onion breaks, may the old woman remain there."

The woman squanders this grace by refusing to share the way out of the burning lake with other sinners, kicking them away, saying "It's my onion, not yours," and so falls back into it as the onion snaps.[60] Yet the grace accompanying her little good

56 Jn 17:21.   57 1 Jn 4:20.   58 Eph 4:32.   59 Jn 1:3.
60 Dostoevsky, *The Karamazov Brothers*, trans. Ignat Avsey (Oxford University Press, 1994), 443–44.

deed could have got her out of the fire if she had accepted it as a means of helping others. Any crack in one's egoism is a way in for universal love or, to put it differently, a way out for the bird of the spirit confined in the egg. If we can be in some way loving towards one person, that gives us the basis for being loving to all: if we find ourselves reacting negatively (even interiorly) to somebody's behavior we can substitute in thought someone for whom we have some sort of positive regard and ask ourselves if we would behave the same way if it were this person doing it. It can even happen that irritation fades away when one turns around and sees that it was not the person one thought making a noise! Love of one enables love of others. Although being in an exclusive marriage might seem to make someone less available to others, my experience has been different: I have in fact oftentimes received more love and attention from people who have dedicated themselves to marriage than from those who have not yet embarked on such a sacred path. Love is undivided.

Love is undividedness, a refusal of the fruit of the tree of the knowledge of good and evil, a giving back to God the judgment that would exclude what is not to our liking. Love is not claiming knowledge about people, for example identifying them with a bad quality or sin, or labeling them. Love is openness and welcoming: if, as Meister Eckhart says, God is distinguished by His indistinction then in making no distinctions between one person and another — in Christ "there is neither male nor female"[61] and so on — we are welcoming Him. Love is the presence of God: "God is love and he that dwelleth in love dwelleth in God, and God in him."[62] Prayer, faith and the love for others issuing from them are the path to His loving presence: "If we love one another, God dwelleth in us, and his love is perfected in us."[63] This is enlightenment, for "he that loveth his brother abideth in the light."[64] This is eternal life, for "He that doeth the will of God abideth for ever."[65] This is what abides forever, so St Paul concludes his great description of love: "And now abideth faith, hope, charity, these three; but the greatest of these is charity."[66] As he describes it, it is mostly a matter of enduring: "Charity suffereth long . . . Beareth all things, believeth all things, hopeth all things, endureth all things."[67] As St Thérèse taught and showed by her undaunted example: "Perfect charity consists in putting up with others' faults and not being at all surprised by their weaknesses, in being edified by the smallest acts of virtue that one sees them practice." Above all, she realized, "Charity shouldn't rest shut up in the bottom of the heart." She understood that it has to radiate to everyone since "No-one, said Jesus, lights a candle to put it under the bushel, but it is put in a candle-stick, so that it lights up all those who are in the house. It seems to me that this candle represents charity which should light up and make happy not only those who are most dear to me, but all those who are in the house, without leaving anyone out."[68] The love we are called to shines undimmed on everyone, since we are all children of the same God: it is both fraternal and abiding. Hence the letter to the Hebrews says, "Let brotherly love continue,"[69] — μενέτω (*menetō*), from μένειν (*menein*), the word that echoes through this book — meaning abide, remain, dwell, as God does in the soul.

Of course this is easier to speak or write about than to do. It is a struggle to win the kingdom and "the violent take it by force."[70] That is an appropriate focus for Tuesday with its association with Mars and the martial and with Tiw and his heroic sacrifice. Battle needs to be undertaken to contemplate the abiding: we need to struggle against the passions which lock our hearts onto the passing things of this world instead of eternal goods. In this context "passion" indicates not a yearning for something good (as in "a passion for justice") but a disordered

---

65 1 Jn 2:17.   66 1 Cor 13:13.   67 1 Cor 13:4,7.

68 *Thérèse de L'Enfant-Jésus*, 250. This, and subsequent citations from St Thérèse, are in my own translation.   69 Heb 13:1.   70 Mt 11:12.

drive towards something not truly beneficial that therefore needs to be resisted. So, for example, in order to have "a treasure in the heavens that faileth not, where no thief approacheth, neither moth corrupteth" it is necessary to struggle to free the heart from the passion of avarice, "for where your treasure is, there will your heart be also."[71] Traditionally, the ascesis of active struggling against disordered passions precedes contemplation. Origen, for example, interprets "Come and see"[72] (the invitation to see where the Lord abides, considered in the previous chapter) as referring to both: "come" indicating the action involved in moral conversion and "see" contemplation.[73] For perfect contemplation, a heart free from passions is needed: "Blessed are the pure in heart: for they shall see God."[74] This isn't to say that there can be no contemplation until there is no impurity in the heart: indeed, contemplation can be a source of purity just as, while one likes to tidy a house before having a guest to stay, some guests are kind enough to help with cleaning and tidying! This is certainly the case for the One who says, "Behold, I stand at the door, and knock: if any man hear my voice, and open the door, I will come in to him, and will sup with him, and he with me."[75] The essential thing is to listen and open up. He cannot (out of His huge respect for us) do that for us, a truth depicted in the celebrated Holman Hunt painting of Him knocking on a door that has no handle on the outside. If we ask Him, He will come in, despite the imperfections of the house, as He came into the house of Zacchaeus, the tax collector.[76] Then, with the help of His grace, an effort can be made to improve the welcome, just as Zacchaeus took a stand against his own avarice by saying to his Guest, "Behold, Lord, the half of my goods I give to the poor; and if I have taken any thing from any man by false accusation, I restore him fourfold."[77] The more we struggle to abide in the Lord — to share the goods that we

71 Lk 12:33–34.   72 Jn 1:38.
73 Cf Borella, *Christ the Original Mystery*, 274.   74 Mt 5:8.
75 Rv 3:20.   76 Lk 19:6–7.   77 Lk 19:8.

would like to keep for ourselves, to bite the tongue that is about to make an uncharitable remark, to think what arrangement is good for others — the more we realize we need Him to abide in us. In His mercy He may let us think for a time that we are taking the initiative in coming to Him, but reality dawns when we realize our own powerlessness to win the war against all that impedes us from entering the eternal abode of undying life until *He* comes to abide in *us* with His great love for us, which is at one and the same time our love for others. With this realization our prayer becomes that of the hymn recalling the encounter of two of His followers with the Lord on the road to Emmaus and their invitation to Him:[78]

> Abide with me; fast falls the eventide;
> The darkness deepens; Lord, with me abide;
> When other helpers fail and comforts flee,
> Help of the helpless, oh, abide with me.[79]

The next chapter looks at His response to this prayer.

---

78 Lk 24:29.   79 Hymn text by Henry Francis Lyte.

CHAPTER FOUR

He dwelleth with you

WEDNESDAY, THE GIFT OF LOVE

*"If a man love me, he will keep my words: and
my Father will love him, and we will come unto
him, and make our abode with him."*[1]

Openness to All

Wednesday is the day of the planet Mercury, named after
the Roman god Mercury, who was seen as both messenger and
mediator. Mercury is 38% of the earth's distance from the sun
and 38% of its size. That proportion is the same as the smaller
portion of the Golden Section, a ratio that appears naturally, as
for example in the human finger where the distance from the
tip to the first joint is 38% of the distance from the tip to the
second joint and these two distances together are 38% of the
distance from the fingertip to the knuckle joint. Mercury, unlike
all the other planets, has an axis that is vertical relative to its
orbit of the sun. It inclines neither one way nor the other. So
Mercury is associated with harmony: its relative position and
size reflect the wholesome working of nature, and its lack of
bias symbolizes an openness to all. Such is Wednesday, inclining
neither to the beginning nor the end of the week, and such was
the god of the ancient Roman world, Mercury, favoring neither
male nor female because androgynous. The day of the week and
its presiding god are linked in *mercredi*, the French name for
it.[2] The Latin name *dies Mercurii* (the day of Mercury) became

---

1 Jn 14:23.   2 Cf Held, *Rhythms of the Week*, 50.

wodnesdæg (Woden's day) in Old English and thence Wednesday.[3] Woden is the Saxon word for the Norse god Odin, identified with Mercury because he is, like him, a psychopomp: a guide for the spirits of those departing this life. Odin has both masculine and feminine qualities, like the androgynous Mercury. His name means "Master of Ecstasy" — he is a poetry god and a dispenser of poetic inspiration.[4]

How do we, who so easily give way to passion and partiality, achieve the balanced position and openness to all that characterize Mercury and live inspired lives of poetic harmony? We have no option but to admit that it is beyond the reach of our own strength. Our own efforts fail us. As the hymn-writer cited in the previous chapter realized, we need to ask for the life-giving presence of the One who does not change:

> Swift to its close ebbs out life's little day;
> Earth's joys grow dim, its glories pass away;
> Change and decay in all around I see —
> O Thou who changest not, abide with me.[5]

We are in the position of Peter in his fishing boat who says, "We have toiled all the night, and have taken nothing."[6] Peter does not give up, however, but responds to the word of the Lord and catches "a great multitude of fishes."[7] It is the dependence on Him that makes the difference. The needed change is encapsulated in the first two of the Twelve Steps in the program of that name for escaping addiction: the admission of a powerlessness and the belief in "a Power greater than ourselves." It is this Power, the Omnipotent, who enables St Francis to kiss the leper, St Teresa of Calcutta to wash the wounds of the poorest of the poor, St Maximilian Kolbe to substitute himself for the family

---

3 https://www.etymonline.com/word/Wednesday#etymonline_v_4884
4 https://norse-mythology.org/gods-and-creatures/the-aesir-gods-and
   -goddesses/odin/
5 Hymn text by Henry Francis Lyte.   6 Lk 5:5.   7 Lk 5:6.

man condemned to death. All of us are more or less addicted
to the self, turned in on ourselves, selfish and need to be saved
from this: "If we say we have no sin, we deceive ourselves, and
the truth is not in us."[8] In our very failure is a grace, for it
opens us to the divine initiative, leads us to pray from the heart,
"Abide in me."[9] Our efforts make us ready to receive the fruit,
the seed of which inspired these efforts. Our struggles to reach
the Divine Physician in His House of Charity make us realize
that we need a home visit from Him. In reality it all begins with
Him. Our prayer comes from His Spirit, "for we know not what
we should pray for as we ought: but the Spirit itself maketh
intercession for us with groanings which cannot be uttered."[10]
Our trust comes from His word, as Peter's trust comes from the
word ("Come")[11] that he gets as an answer to his request, "Lord,
if it be thou, bid me come unto thee on the water."[12] Our deeds
of love, truly understood, can only be duly credited in the words
of the psalm, "Not unto us, O LORD, not unto us, but unto thy
name give glory, for thy mercy, and for thy truth's sake."[13]

God Abiding in Us

Love invites the Divine Physician to visit our sickbed, but
"Herein is love, not that we loved God, but that he loved us."[14]
And wonderfully, what begins as an emergency call-out ends as an
abiding presence, for the Lord tells us "If a man love me, he will
keep my words and my Father will love him, and we will come
unto him, and make our abode with him."[15] His love for us is the
beginning of our loving Him; His example the inspiration for our
keeping His words; His abiding in us the reward of them both.
In the progress towards sanctity, that abiding goes on to sideline
the self so that it is no longer linked to vitality: hence St Paul
can say, "not I, but Christ liveth in me."[16] This life of Christ in
the saint is the inner, essential life of all since "without him was

8 1 Jn 1:8. 9 Jn 15:4. 10 Rom 8:26. 11 Mt 14:29.
12 Mt 14:28. 13 Ps 115:1. 14 1 Jn 4:10. 15 Jn 14:23.
16 Gal 2:20.

not any thing made that was made."[17] It is therefore the universal life designated by the words at the beginning of John's gospel "In him was life,"[18] the giving of which is spoken of by the Lord as His mission: "I am come that they might have life and have it more abundantly."[19] It is the life of the Christian. For the one living it to the full, relations with others are radically different from those undertaken from a selfish perspective. It is not just that such a person will be more helpful, though obviously that will usually be the case, for "faith, if it hath not works, is dead, being alone."[20] Those who encounter such a person will instinctively and intuitively recognize his or her life as being their own, for at the deepest level it is: Christ is the One in whom we have life. This is more than companionship: it is a transcendence of separation. The life of such a person, even one who is too old and infirm to undertake active works, is an expansion of everybody's life. Nor is the impression the saintly make primarily through the persuasiveness of their reasoning: it is simply from the life lived in them. That does not mean that everyone will appreciate them — there are those at war with their deepest self who say, "Let us lie in wait for the righteous man, because he is inconvenient to us and opposes our actions,"[21] but responsiveness to this universal life will be widespread. There is no barrier of egotism. In the words of the third Eucharistic Prayer, folk become "one body, one spirit in Christ." This is the fulfillment of the Lord's priestly prayer "That they all may be one; as thou, Father, art in me, and I in thee, that they also may be one in us."[22]

With the Father and the Son abides also "the Spirit of truth" who the Lord says, "dwelleth with you, and shall be in you."[23] With the anointing of the Spirit comes wisdom, living and enduring, for "the anointing which ye have received of him abideth in you, and ye need not that any man teach you: but as the same anointing teacheth you of all things, and is truth, and is

17 Jn 1:3.   18 Jn 1:3.   19 Jn 10:10.   20 Jas 2:17.
21 Ws 2:12 (Revised Standard Version).   22 Jn 17:21.   23 Jn 14:17.

no lie, and even as it hath taught you, ye shall abide in him."²⁴
The words rendered by "dwelleth" and "abideth" are forms of the
Greek verb μένειν (*menein*) with the implication both of life and
of enduring. In question is nothing less than the life of the Holy
Trinity—Father, Son and Holy Spirit—the eternal life of God
in which we participate through His indwelling. The Holy Spirit
incorporates us into the Body of Christ, the Church, for the
Spirit is the life and soul of the Church. It is He who leads us as
disciples to come and see where Christ abides for "no man can
say that Jesus is the Lord but by the Holy Ghost."²⁵ God abiding
in us leads us to abide in God. Inwardly that abiding in us is the
Holy Spirit with His grace coming to us that we may come to
Christ; outwardly it is God coming among us when "the Word
was made flesh and dwelt among us."²⁶ The Holy Spirit enables
us to recognize that coming among us, continued in the sacra-
ments and teaching of the Church and the words of Scripture.

God always wants to abide in us. As He says to the tax gath-
erer Zacchaeus, so He says to us: "to day I must abide at thy
house."²⁷ He wants to dwell, to live and stay, with us: all that
is implied by the verb μένειν (*menein*). It is a temptation of the
devil to keep Him out while we clean the house, as St Teresa
of Ávila—the great teacher of prayer—was tempted for a time
not to pray because "it showed a lack of humility to persist"
on account of her wickedness.²⁸ He is not put off entering the
house of Zacchaeus on account of his being "a man that is a
sinner,"²⁹ nor is He put off by the fact that "the Jews have no
dealings with the Samaritans"³⁰ from responding to the request
"that he would tarry with them" for "he abode there two days."³¹
"Tarry" and "abode" again render a form of μένειν (*menein*), sig-
naling an eternal and living presence. Necessarily that presence
has to come to us before we are worthy of it; the Incarnation
did not depend on a triumphal welcome into Jerusalem being

24 1 Jn 2:27.   25 1 Cor 12:3.   26 Jn 1:14.   27 Lk 19:5.
28 *The Life of Saint Teresa of Ávila by Herself*, trans. J.M. Cohen (London:
Penguin, 1958), 130.   29 Lk 19:7.   30 Jn 4:9.   31 Jn 4:40.

the only response to it and nor does the indwelling of God in us depend on us having a record free of blemish, to put it mildly. The truth is that, like water bubbling irrepressibly out of the ground, like air coming into a vacuum, like a mother feeding her child, God wants His life to be in us. "The love of God is shed abroad in our hearts by the Holy Ghost which is given unto us"[32] and that love is no less than a wish to share His very life with us through the One who promises "because I live, ye shall live also."[33] This pledge goes on to echo the telling of the disciples' first encounter with Him: "At that day ye shall know that I am in the Father, and ye in me, and I in you"[34] for it is the same day alluded to in the first chapter of the gospel in which we are told that they "abode with him that day."[35] It is the eternal day, the fullness of God's life manifested in the resurrection which shows us eternity in the flesh. In knowing that the Lord Jesus is in the Father we see where He abides; in knowing that we are in Him and He in us we discover the grace-given fulfillment of His word, which tells us "Abide in me, and I in you"[36] and gives us the power to do and receive this; knowing all of this — that He is in the Father, and we in Him, and He in us — changes who we are. In our awareness and embrace of the indescribable blessing of God's indwelling in us we become what the seventeenth-century Benedictine teacher of contemplation Augustine Baker calls "inward livers" — people who live from the unfathomable mystery of God within. This is indefectible life, for "the Son abideth for ever."[37] It is the fulfillment of the Lord's promise of the eternal presence of the Spirit: "And I will pray the Father, and he shall give you another Comforter that he may be with you for ever."[38] He offers us "the power of an endless life."[39] This is the life of the Holy Trinity: the Son abiding in us, and so the Father also, and the Spirit of them both gifted to us.

32 Rom 5:5.   33 Jn 14:19.   34 Jn 14:20.   35 Jn 1:39.
36 Jn 15:4.   37 Jn 8:35.   38 Jn 14:16.   39 Heb 7:16.

The Key to the Heart

This talk of God bringing life by coming to abide in us is of course a metaphor, for God transcends space as He transcends time. We can equally aptly say that Christ, being the very principle of our existence, is already within and we in our outward-facing lives ignore His gentle presence until we learn to find Him there. Such is the metaphor of Teresa of Ávila's treatise *The Interior Castle*. She envisages the Lord being in the steadfast keep at the center of the soul. The early stages of the spiritual life are spent in the outer precincts of the castle where there are dangerous reptiles. These are temptations to sin. Only in the center of the castle does their diabolic instigator lack all sway. The move to the interior is the pilgrimage to holiness so that, for example, resentments that are not easily let go of in the more outward parts of the castle melt away as one comes into the presence of the Lord of love. The same move from the outward to the inner is chronicled in St Augustine's *Confessions*. In his search for God he interrogates the sky, the sun, the moon and the stars that he sees above him and they answer that they are not God but that He made them.[40] He ranges widely through the capacity of the human memory and realizes it reaches beyond even those things we have already known to blessedness itself.[41] He says to God, "You abide in my memory."[42] He reflects on his quest, "You were within, and I was outside and searched for you there."[43]

These metaphors of pilgrimage and search speak aptly of an inner presence already there, but they fail to convey the truth that our coming to this place is God's work rather than our own. It is not so much the case that we find Christ in our inmost being as that He unlocks our heart from within. In the liturgy of Advent He is identified as the Key: there we sing in an antiphon for the Magnificat, "*O Clavis David*" (O Key of David). This alludes to the Book of Revelation, which speaks of "he that is holy, he that

40 *Confessions*, Book 10, Chapter 6.   41 *Confessions*, Chapters 8–23.
42 *Confessions*, Chapter 24.   43 *Confessions*, Chapter 27.

is true, he that hath the key of David."[44] As such, He is able to say, "I have set before thee an open door, and no man can shut it."[45] He is our Liberator, for he has "the keys of hell and of death"[46] and is able to give us a share in the vision of "his servant John"[47] who testified, "I looked, and, behold, a door was opened in heaven."[48] The Lord Jesus is the Key to our heart: through His tender love He unlocks it; thus unlocked it is open to loving others and so to the self-forgetfulness that is, ultimately, heaven.

G.K. Chesterton develops the idea of the creed, which teaches us faith in Christ, as a key: "the key that could unlock the prison of the whole world; and let in the daylight of liberty." Its promulgation was the answer to the problem that "the world had not only got into a hole, but had got into a whole maze of holes and corners." If there was "much about the key that seemed complex," there was "one thing about it that was simple. It opened the door."[49] The faith of the creed enables us to know the Key of David. He unlocks from within the prison of fear as "when the doors were shut where the disciples were assembled for fear" and He "saith unto them, Peace be unto you"[50] and empowers them to speak "the word of God with boldness"[51] and set people free from their sins.[52] He unlocks from within the dungeon of doubt, as when "the doors being shut" He said to the disciples again "Peace be unto you" and to Thomas, "Reach hither thy finger, and behold my hands; and reach hither thy hand, and thrust it into my side: and be not faithless but believing." He unlocks the heart to make Thomas' humble admission of faith, "My Lord and my God."[53]

The one who allows himself to be unlocked from within comes to know an essential identity which has nothing to do with power or possessions, with empire or achievement, with status or success. It is simply the realization of the promise to

---

44 Rv 3:7.   45 Rv 3:8.   46 Rv 1:18.   47 Rv 1:1.   48 Rv 4.1
49 G.K. Chesterton, *The Everlasting Man*, Part 2, Section 4 (New York: Dover, 2007).
50 Jn 20:19.   51 Acts 4:31.   52 Jn 20:22–23.   53 Jn 20:26–28.

the one who overcomes the superficialities of the outer self: "I will write upon him the name of my God."[54] This is a sharing in the identity of God. And since God sources and sustains all that is, it is an identification with the essence of all of creation. It is a oneness with all of life that cannot be wrested away, for it is the life of the One by whom "all things were made."[55] It is eternal life, for it is the life of the One who is "the way, the truth, and the life"[56] and "the resurrection, and the life."[57] It is the life of the One who has come that we might have life, and that we might have it "more abundantly"[58] — an abundance which is nothing less than a participation in God's own life, making us "partakers of the divine nature."[59]

Receiving or Refusing Life and Truth

This life is, as we saw in the last chapter, received through faith. We simply need to allow it remain in us as St John exhorts: "Let that therefore abide (μενέτω/*menetō*) in you which ye have heard from the beginning. If that which ye have heard from the beginning shall remain (μείνῃ/*meine*) in you, ye also shall continue (μενεῖτε/*meneite*) in the Son, and in the Father."[60] Through allowing the word we have heard to remain, we allow the Word made flesh to remain. The various forms of the verb μένειν (*menein*) emphasize that His presence is eternal. The phrase "from the beginning" echoes the beginning of the gospel of John, "In the beginning was the Word"[61] and the beginning of the Bible, "In the beginning God created the heaven and the earth."[62] The "beginning" is not just the point at which we first received the faith — which faith has remained the same ever since — it is also the first moment of creation, the eternal now from which everything blossomed forth. The word of faith comes from that primordial moment and enables us to realize the presence of Him by whom "all things were made,"[63] He who

---

54 Rv 3:12.   55 Jn 1:3.   56 Jn 14.6.   57 Jn 11:25.   58 Jn 10:10.
59 2 Pt 1:4.   60 1 Jn 2:24.   61 Jn 1:1.   62 Gn 1:1.   63 Jn 1:3.

"was in the beginning with God."[64] The eternal source—before, or better, beyond time—ensures that "the word of God abideth (μένει/ *menei*)" in us.[65] Because its source is eternal and primordial, the word we have heard is always alive, ever ancient, ever new, as fresh as the first creation. The revelation is not back then, now gathering dust in its distance from our time: it is given life in the very moment. The teaching of the truth comes from Christ in the gospel; the teaching of us now from the Holy Spirit, as He explains: "These things have I spoken unto you, being yet present with you. But the Comforter, which is the Holy Ghost, which the Father will send in my name, he shall teach you all things, and bring all things to your remembrance, whatsoever I have said unto you."[66] This is not simply addressed to the first disciples, who were there as Christ spoke and are to have their memories of His teaching awakened, it is addressed now to His disciples in the depths of whose spirit lies the truth to be awakened by the sacred word and the Holy Ghost. This truth is there like a sleeping princess in the neglected steadfastness of our interiority whose helplessness dumbly cries out to the Prince of Peace, "Let him kiss me with the kisses of his mouth."[67] She longs to be aroused and say, "We will be glad and rejoice in thee."[68]

The life we have in Christ depends on this truth. The health of our holiness depends on its active presence. Spiritual life is analogous to physical life. The life of the body depends on certain truths: a wisdom about what exercise to take, what to eat or drink, when and how long to rest, what perils to avoid and so on. In a similar way, eternal life depends on the teaching of Christ handed down to us and vivified by "the Spirit of truth" who will guide us "into all truth."[69] This sets before us "life and good, death and evil."[70] The New Moses echoes the patriarch's exhortation, "Choose life."[71] However, it can be refused. Because

64 Jn 1:2.   65 1 Jn 2:14.   66 Jn 14:25–26.   67 Sg 1:2.
68 Sg 1:4.   69 Jn 16:13.   70 Dt 30:15.   71 Dt 30:19.

it depends on receiving and giving love (and love is not true love if it is not given freely) eternal life (a life that cannot die because in it we are in communion with the very heart of being and so with all that is) can be refused. Scripture is very clear about this. We can either trust "the way, the truth, and the life"[72] or not trust: "He that believeth on the Son hath everlasting life: and he that believeth not the Son shall not see life; but the wrath of God abideth on him."[73] This is not an injunction to engage in narrow religious identity politics; it is saying that: there is a way to live that leads to life, there is a truth about who we are that we ignore at our peril — we have been shown these and invited to live life to the full. We have been told, "He that loveth not his brother abideth (μένει / *menei*) in death. Whosoever hateth his brother is a murderer: and ye know that no murderer hath eternal life abiding (μένουσαν / *menousan*) in him..."[74] This is a universal truth. Love and abiding life are inseparable, for love is the presence of the eternal God and if one "hath this world's good, and seeth his brother have need, and shutteth up his bowels of compassion from him, how dwelleth (μένει / *menei*) the love of God in him?"[75] And without the love of God, what is there for us when we go to Him? Death can abide as well as life. So can sin: it is the concomitant of the claim to know that the confession of faith is wrong — "If ye were blind, ye should have no sin: but now ye say, We see; therefore your sin remaineth (μένει / *menei*)."[76] It is not doubt or uncertainty that is sin. Indeed the light of truth is shed into our hearts rather when we do not prejudge what it will show us. As Simone Weil well observed, "It is when we desire truth with an empty soul and without attempting to guess its content that we receive the light."[77] Sin is the certainty of thinking we know when we do not: its essence is the primal sin of pride. And that excludes the light of truth and so excludes abiding life: "Whosoever

---

72 Jn 14:6.   73 Jn 3:26.   74 1 Jn 3:14–15.   75 1 Jn 3:17.   76 Jn 9:41.
77 Simone Weil, *On the Abolition of All Political Parties* (New York Review of Books Classics, 2014), 21–22.

committeth sin is the servant of sin. And the servant abideth (μένει/ *menei*) not in the house for ever."[78]

This choice is stark because of God's great respect for us. He wants us to be free, for our life to be in some sense of our making, because he wants us to have nothing less than the incomparable joy of really loving. Wednesday is the mid-point of the week as its German name *Mittwoch* asserts. This is the middle of the middle (and longest) chapter of this book. It is the hinge. Everything turns on this. Do we accept this light, this love, this life which God so lovingly offers us through His Christ?

God's Prayer

Any yes to this question is the whisper of the Spirit of God blowing gently through the leaves of the trees in the forest of our psyche; it is water bubbling up in the parched land of our soul; it is a prayer that, though it seems to come from us, is the gift of God, gifting us to receive the only gift that He deems good enough for us: His own self, His very life. Prayer is the way we receive the gift and though it is an enterprise that we undertake (as considered in the previous chapter) ultimately it becomes the work of God worked for us, the life of God worked in our souls: a life that was hidden in our earliest efforts but that comes more into view as we realize that "we know not what we should pray for as we ought" and "the Spirit itself maketh intercession for us."[79] Our abiding in God through prayer comes about through God's prayer abiding in us, through God in us.

The dynamic of this work of God in the soul becoming manifest and full is traced by St Teresa of Ávila in her *Life*. She sees prayer in terms of water, a symbol of the Spirit. The first stage is getting water from a well. This expresses the laboriousness of the beginnings of a spiritual life. The effort involved is in reaching down to the depth of the soul, where God is. To change the metaphor for a moment it is as though we have a guest staying

<hr />

78 Jn 8:34–35.   79 Rom 8:26.

in our home but we are nearly always out and have to make an effort to get back from time to time. The start of the Lord's abiding is His host spending some time indoors. The second stage is getting water with a windlass (a device for pulling up water receptacles with a wheel). Here it may be supposed that going within the soul is a regular habit no longer requiring special effort. In the third stage there is "water flowing from a stream or spring." Now the Lord "does everything."[80] The soul is no longer alienated from herself and finds her life within where the Lord is. The water in the fourth stage is "rain that comes down abundantly from heaven."[81] Here the soul may be supposed to be living wholly within, so much so that touching the immanent presence of God there she knows also His transcendence and so goes beyond herself to fully share His life. The one who used to be thought of as a guest is now a resident. This is the end of her earthly journey which started with efforts (as described in the last chapter) to abide in God. She ends where she begins; the transformation is that now it is God working, not her. Beyond this there is paradise where prayer is no longer affected by the gravity of the fall, as when "there went up a mist from the earth, and watered the whole face of the ground."[82] I have not followed St Teresa exactly here, but rather have used her metaphors to indicate the interplay of human and divine work in the soul's progress towards a mutual indwelling.[83] The essential point is that it is finally the work of the Lord.

The essence of His prayer, which is sometimes referred to as His high priestly prayer, is recorded for us in Chapter 17 of St John's gospel. This ends with the purpose of His declaration of the Father's name: "that the love wherewith thou hast loved me may be in them, and I in them."[84] This love is the Holy Spirit which is also the Spirit of truth, for loving and knowing are finally the

---

80 *Life of Saint Teresa of Ávila*, 112.   81 *Life of Saint Teresa of Ávila*, 125.
82 Gn 2:6.
83 The four stages are outlined in *Life of Saint Teresa of Ávila*, 78, and explained more fully in Chapters 11–19.   84 Jn 17:26.

same. Hence the Lord prays, "Sanctify them through thy truth."[85] The loving and the knowing are one; the loving and the being loved are one; the knowing and the being known are one. They are simply the Holy Spirit, which the Lord bestowed with His last breath when He "gave up the ghost."[86] His prayer to the Father is that through that Spirit "they all may be one; as thou, Father art in me, and I in thee, that they also may be one in us."[87] The Spirit integrates us so that we become indeed what we ask to become in the canon of the Mass: "one body, one Spirit in Christ."[88]

Love

The love, the Spirit that makes us one, comes from God: "Herein is love, not that we loved God, but that he loved us."[89] The Spirit, not we ourselves, makes us holy, makes us loving. "God commendeth his love toward us, in that, while we were yet sinners, Christ died for us."[90] We do not need to hide ourselves or our talents because His mercy, not our worthiness, is the way to dwelling in His love. Everywhere, the Scripture speaks of it. We can only pray, "Remember, O LORD, thy tender mercies and thy lovingkindnesses; for they have been ever of old"[91] and "Have mercy upon me, O God, according to thy lovingkindness: according to the multitude of thy tender mercies blot out my transgressions."[92] Our God is "plenteous in mercy"[93] and "the dayspring from on high hath visited us" through His "tender mercy."[94] That is what makes possible His abiding in us. If we allow this, we become tender like Him. In that staying, He in us and we in Him, we become tender, slow-cooked as it were in the warmth of His love; we are transformed in love. Humbly accepting our weakness, as He humbly accepted that same weakness, we rely on Him, not ourselves. Peter had no staying power when he relied on himself, but became indeed a rock when he relied

---

85 Jn 17:7.   86 Jn 19:30.   87 Jn 17:21.
88 Third Eucharistic Prayer, Roman Missal.   89 1 Jn 4:10.
90 Rom 5:8.   91 Ps 25:6.   92 Ps 51:1.   93 Ps 103:8.   94 Lk 1:78.

on God, the rock he was named to be.[95] Peter, as leader, is every
Christian, and we are all called to such a reliance as his. Unity in
tender and merciful love comes from a reliance on God's promise: "And I will give them one heart, and I will put a new spirit
within you; and I will take their stony heart out of their flesh,
and will give them an heart of flesh."[96] It is not angelism, living
as though we were pure spirit, that God wants of us, but that
we should make the journey from the head to the heart, to our
human heart, to the supremely human heart, to the Sacred and
Human Heart of Our Lord and Savior Jesus Christ.

That journey can start with ordinary human affections. St Aelred
of Rivaulx wrote of an ascent *de Christo amorem inspirante quo
amicum diligimus* — by Christ inspiring the love with which we
love a friend.[97] To love someone truly is to want to love that person better, and so it is to turn to Christ whose love is divine: at
once truly abiding and truly tender. The divine love can give what
we want to give the one we love but on our own cannot. A heart
opened by love for another is open to receive this love that says,
"As the Father hath loved me, so have I loved you."[98] A heart that
wants to remain true can do so by obeying the injunction that
follows these words: "continue (μείνατε / *meinate*) ye in my love."[99]
We naturally love particular people and we therefore are given
Christ in particular. He is the absolute particular, the Unique who
gives each person his or her uniqueness — the absolutely unique
from which comes the relative uniqueness of each of us. So in loving any particular person we are given (love for another is a gift)
an instantiation of that perfect love which is the fullness of charity:
love of the Lord who holds all people to His Sacred Heart as brothers and sisters. And the challenge is this: to enter into the heart
of this love that we have for a particular person and find therein
that which it instantiates. To do that is to reach the very fullness of
communion: that love in which everyone is very dear and special.

95 Cf Mt 16:18.   96 Ez 11:19.   97 *De Spirituali Amicitia*, Book Two.
98 Jn 15:9.   99 Jn 15:9.

The reason this is challenging is that it can seem that if everyone is unique in this way then no one is, that the special enhancement of life that comes from gathering another into how we know things (with its concomitant deepening of our engagement with reality) will somehow be lost or diminished. It looks like spreading love so thin that it no longer has depth. Yet that is not so. This is an outward and quantitative view of the matter. In fact by entering into the heart of the particular we find the Particular ("this Jesus")[100] who is at the heart of every particular. We lose the outward life that grasps only that which is relatively special and gain the inward life that is absolutely special. We find uniqueness and particularity in its fullness. We become "children of light,"[101] having that light of knowing with which God truly knows and loves each person.

How human love opens us to becoming enlightened in this way is beautifully caught in this poem:

> I wanted to write something about Oxford skies
> The way they seemed from your window,
>   and when I was young
> Contemplating the skyline from a sickbed
> And realised — I'd never slept in Oxford
>
> Except with you — or in short fever dreams
> From which I had hated to return
> Those brief glimpses of eternity
> I would later lust for and not find
>
> But you have opened up your curtains to me
> Bringing the world with you into my arms
> And though I am poor, now I own everything
> And cannot lose or be lost, even if I lost you
>
> Touched once by light I was long lost
> Touched once by you is found forever

100 Acts 2:32.   101 Eph 5:8.

The poem is called *Skylight*.[102] The title refers to the window through which the light comes, the light of the sky that comes through it and the light of heaven of which this is a symbol. The first stanza describes seeing the light literally in a particular place, the second the intuition of eternal light, once had and now lost, and the third a particular person as a skylight through which that light is received. She brings "the world" into the poet's arms for, like every soul, she contains and communicates it. In the speaker's transcendence of possession ("I am poor") there is ownership of "everything." This is the final enlightenment, a going beyond losing or being lost. Remarkably, this transcends even the possible eventuality of the loss of the beloved: universal love is found, the poet attests to his beloved, "even if I lost you." In the final couplet, there is a reprise of the whole: the first experience of finding and losing the light and then enlightenment through being touched by one's love, an enlightenment that in the end reveals itself not as a questing but as a being sought, ultimately not a human but a divine initiative. Because "you" in the final line is in apposition to "light" (as in Christ's identification of Himself as "the light of the world"),[103] in the previous line, "touched once by you" indicates a saving encounter with Him, hidden as it were within the "you" of the loved one. God's love draws us through our human love.

When we see the love we have for a particular person as what it is on the deepest plane, see the inward reality that it outwardly shows, we have it in its essence. Love is never an abstraction; we become loving through loving particular people. And that particular love can lead us to universal love. Seeking the steadfastness and depth of this love in our loving we are drawn to Christ and turning to Him we touch the One in whom all have their deepest being; loving Him we love everyone in their deepest selves.

102 From a forthcoming collection by Sam Davidson. Used by permission.
103 Jn 8:12, 9:5.

Tenderness is transferable. Really to love another is to love Christ, that person's deepest Self, and so to love everyone: indeed it is to love everything, as it happens and the way it happens since "all things were made by him; and without him was not anything made that was made."[104] This is spiritual love; its intimacy is closer than that of love of other sorts, though it can be within other sorts of love. God is closer to us than we are to ourselves, and so in God we have that sort of intimacy with others. We see with the eyes of the Spirit those we pray for. We touch dear ones in prayer. Consecrated celibacy has a special reach here. John Milton wrote of "the sun-clad power of chastity."[105] Its love is like the sun because the sun's light and warmth reach everywhere: its love is in God and God is everywhere present.

And it changes everything. In loving Christ we love God. And as love of a particular person makes special the city in which that person lives, so love of God changes the whole of creation for it all speaks of Him: the lion of His majesty, the dove of His peacefulness, the peacock of His beauty and so on. Most particularly, people speak of Him. Each person holds the whole of creation in his or her thoughts. Each person is an image of the Creator's presence in His creation. To love God is to love that presence; it is to love those people and their apprehension of the Creation; it is to love creation afresh. Love changes everybody. To love a person is to change that person: in one's own eyes first — annoying habits become endearing foibles, for example — and maybe in their eyes also as in the princess kissing the frog and transforming him by her love into a prince. Love changes our difficulties. Labor undertaken out of love becomes a joy. Doing things for God "makes drudgery divine."[106] Love changes suffering so that it becomes an

---

104 Jn 1:3.

105 *A Masque Presented at Ludlow Castle, 1634* [*Comus*], line 781, in *John Milton, Complete Shorter Poems* ed. John Carey (Harlow, UK: Longman, 1971), 215.

106 "The Elixer," line 18, in *The English Poems of George Herbert*, ed. C.A. Patrides (London: Dent, 1974), 188.

expression of love. Such love brings joy, so St Thérèse was able to say of anything, however dark: *"j'en fais ma joie"* — I make my joy of it. Suffering offered up becomes a source of blessing, as when St Teresa Benedicta of the Cross (Edith Stein) went to Auschwitz for her people, following in the footsteps of the Savior, a sacrifice given poetic expression by James Wilson:

> What terrible love did she bear?
> The soldiers massed about the steeple,
> Breaking the sisters from their prayer?
> "Come, we are going for our people."

> Pressed in the rattling cattle car
> Between her sister and rough board,
> Drawn through the final smoke of war?
> "Come, we are going to our Lord."[107]

St Teresa Benedicta understood the deep wisdom of the first and great commandment, "Thou shalt love the Lord thy God with all thy heart, and with all thy soul, and with all thy mind."[108] St John of the Cross, who also understood, wrote: "At the evening of life, you will be examined in love."[109] This is a fair judgment because it does not depend on our abilities, only the love with which we acted and suffered. The way to be happy is to receive and respond to God's love. God is our love, our eternal happiness and peace. He wants to give Himself to us. The next chapter considers the particular way in which He does this.

107　"Some Will Remember You" in *The Hanging God: Poems by James Matthew Wilson* (Brooklyn: Angelico Press, 2018), 76.

108　Mt 22:37–38.

109　Sayings of Light and Love, No. 57, *Collected Works of St. John of the Cross*, 672.

CHAPTER FIVE

unto the end

THURSDAY, REAL PRESENCE

"He that eateth my flesh, and drinketh my blood, dwelleth in me, and I in him."[1]

Thor's Day

"Thursday" comes from the Old English *þurresdæg*, a contraction of *þunresdæg*, literally "Thor's day." The Norse god Thor was identified with the Roman god Jupiter whence the name of the planet.[2] Thor's wife, Sif, is noted above all else for her golden hair, evoking the fecundity of fields of ripe grain. Their marriage is one between heaven and earth, he a sky god and she an earth goddess.[3] The wedding of the divine and the earthly, as represented by the harvested fruit of the earth, is celebrated in Christian tradition in the Eucharist, whose day is above all Thursday, for that was the day of the Last Supper. This is the sacrament that makes real the presence of the abiding love that the last two chapters have discussed.

The Sacrament of Communion

I have written of mutual indwelling and love as a spiritual reality but of course it is also a physical reality: in Holy Communion, a communion established by Our Lord Jesus going to the place of exclusion. He leaves communion to bring us into communion.

---

1 Jn 6:56.
2 https://www.etymonline.com/word/Thursday#etymonline_v_13286
3 https://norse-mythology.org/gods-and-creatures/the-aesir-gods-and
   -goddesses/thor/

He allows Himself to be abandoned by those who sleep in the Garden of Gethsemane while He accepts the burden of humanity's separation from its Source. He accepts the shame and outlawing of punishment outside the city wall. He dies for us. And His lack of communion — expressed in the prayer from the Psalter, "My God, my God, why hast thou forsaken me?"[4] — becomes our communion. Dying, He breathes forth His Holy Spirit, in whom we know communion; God's love for us, the Holy Spirit, is our love for others and for Him. This best gift is offered to us wherever we are: God becomes present in humanity's isolation so that His communion reaches even there. The cross gives us the Eucharist. This is a physical spiritual communion, for the Lord has promised: "He that eateth my flesh, and drinketh my blood, dwelleth (μένει/ *menei*) in me and I in him."[5] This is a "hard saying."[6] Yet it is no more hard than saying the Word was made flesh, that the Son of God walked among us. Heaven comes to us where we are, in all the desolation of that place, so that we may go to heaven. We are offered a dwelling, an abiding that goes beyond this world, and invited to "labour not for the meat which perisheth, but for that meat which endureth (μένουσαν/ *menousan*) unto everlasting life."[7] Communion is explicitly this when it is given as viaticum to a person nearing the end of his or her life. Communion takes us from the transitory to the eternal; it is also the eternal enduring among the transitory; it is the fulfillment of the Lord's promise, "Lo, I am with you alway, even unto the end of the world."[8] It is the Lord loving "his own . . . in the world . . . unto the end."[9] In its orientation to eternity, St John the contemplative speaks for it; in its bringing of eternity among us, St Peter the leader speaks for it.

Both of them were there, that first Thursday when the sacrament of the Eucharist, the embodiment of the indwelling of God, source of universal love, was inaugurated. They both heard the

---

4 Mt 27:46, Ps 22:1.   5 Jn 6:56.   6 Jn 6:60.   7 Jn 6:27.
8 Mt 28:20.   9 Jn 13:1.

words, "Take, eat: this is my body, which is broken for you: this
do in remembrance of me."[10] Thursday is the day *par excellence*
for our remembrance of this gift of embodied abiding, our communion with the eternal. It is also the day of Jupiter, the largest
planet, and so of fullness: through the Eucharist we have the
fullness of life. Jupiter is something like twelve times the diam-
eter of the earth and twelve times slower in its orbit of the sun.
The twelve disciples signify the fullness of the Church. Through
their gathering around the Lord in the Last Supper the Church,
prefigured by the twelve tribes of Israel, is formed. In that sacrament we abide in communion with Him and He abides with us.
He is really and abidingly present in both His humanity and His
divinity to the end, giving Himself to us in unreserved love. It is
a presence that we need come rain or sun, as the hymn declares:

> I need Thy presence every passing hour;
> What but Thy grace can foil the tempter's pow'r?
> Who, like Thyself, my guide and stay can be?
> Through cloud and sunshine, Lord, abide with me.[11]

He is our "stay" in both the sense of being a support and in
the sense of remaining with us. His is a presence that guides
us through the promptings His Spirit gives our hearts. His is
a presence so intimate that we actually receive into our bodies
His life and love.

The Presence of Jesus

Receiving Him, "the true bread from heaven . . . he which
cometh down from heaven and giveth life to the world," [12] we
are invited to abide in this love and be set free by the truth of
His word.[13] It is not simply by receiving communion that we
abide in the presence of the Lord, but also by being present to

10 1 Cor 11:24.   11 Hymn text by Henry Francis Lyte.
12 Jn 6:32–33.   13 Cf Jn 8:32.

Him in the Blessed Sacrament, whether exposed on the altar or in the tabernacle. That being present to Him is transformative. I have witnessed this. Towards the end of the last century I had care of a country parish. For the first year that was simply an unremarkable duty. Then we introduced exposition of the Blessed Sacrament for an hour before each of the main Masses, the Saturday evening Mass and the Sunday morning Mass. People would pray there before Mass. That was the point at which things began to change in the parish and it became alive; there was a sense that something was happening in it; it was being transformed. Earlier this century we had an event in my monastery organized by Youth 2000. I had been involved with this organization at the time of my rural ministry. Young people would gather in the Catholic church at Glastonbury and they would be present in front of the Blessed Sacrament; they would go to confession; the time would be transformative for them. At the event in the monastery church the young people were present practically all night; afterwards they gave testimonies about how their hearts were changed, about how they received healing, speaking very openly and impressively. A third example of the transforming presence of the Blessed Sacrament which stays in my mind, though I was not personally present, was in 2010 when Pope Benedict came to England and there was a big event in Hyde Park in London. People were saying that he didn't have the theatrical skills that his predecessor had, that although he was a wise and holy man, perhaps he could not communicate with the crowds in the way Pope St John Paul II could. Yet what happened there was extraordinary. The focus wasn't on Pope Benedict; the focus was on the exposed Blessed Sacrament, before which thousands and thousands of people in the park kept silent vigil. These three examples have one thing in common: Jesus was present. He was present in the church, transforming the life of the parish; he was present in the abbey, transforming the lives of young people; he was present in the park, transforming the life of the nation, changing what was expected to be somewhat of a disaster from the public relations point of view into a time of blessing.

Let us reflect a little on that presence. It is a continuation of the Incarnation: a personal presence that remains as promised even to the end.[14] That means that when we talk about the Eucharist and the Blessed Sacrament, we are also talking about Mary who is as it were the tabernacle. The "yes" of Mary to the Angel Gabriel is a yes that echoes through eternity.[15] Therefore she is spiritually present when Jesus is present in the Blessed Sacrament. It is her openness to God that makes possible the yes, the nothing but yes, that we have in Christ.[16] His yes to us blossoms in our yes to life and what it sends us, in our yes to others, and to Him. His presence affirming us and the affirmation we give comes through Mary. Jesus incarnate through her is in the Blessed Sacrament. The feast of Corpus Christi, when we celebrate that presence, is like having Christmas in the summer.

In both of those great feasts we celebrate Jesus among us. In the former the emphasis is on His sharing our life; in the latter it is on our sharing His life. In our communion with Him, we "live no longer for ourselves but for him."[17] As that communion deepens, our life becomes His and He lives in us. Since He identifies Himself with the least of His brethren[18] — especially those in need — our life includes that of all of humanity. Its subject, its self as it were, is no longer the separated individual but everybody. Our respect for all is our self-respect; our love for all is our flourishing; our care for all is the safe-guarding of our spiritual destiny. In our communion we recognize "our fellowship . . . with the Father, and with his Son Jesus Christ"[19] and our fellowship with all of humanity. The Eucharist is the sacrament of the Incarnation, the wedding of God and Man, and it creates the Church, gathered in the name of Jesus and exemplifying the oneness in love that God among us bestows. The Church is the

14 Cf. Mt 28:20.   15 Cf Lk 1:38.   16 Cf 1 Cor 1:20.
17 Fourth Eucharistic Prayer, Roman Missal.   18 Mt 25:40.   19 1 Jn 1:3.

abiding of the Lord's incarnation, with power to smash down the gates of hell to liberate prisoners of isolation.[20] It is yeast in the dough of humanity to make out of the grains of individuality a companionship in the bread of life. It is a herald of the unity of humanity, saying to all and sundry, "Whither thou goest, I will go; and where thou lodgest, I will lodge: thy people shall be my people, and thy God my God."[21] The message is that God is the God of all, not "ours" — and still less "mine" — as opposed to "yours" for God is united to humanity as such in the Incarnation. Through the Incarnation our family transcends our tribe, our race and indeed the grouping of those who share our beliefs or religious practices. It expands our life beyond measure. For God, however, it is a different story.

Christ Accepting Limitation and Giving the Spirit

For God, the Incarnation is, to put it essentially, accepting limitation. As Saint Cyril of Alexandria put it, "When he became man, he made the limitations of humanity his own."[22] This is a delicacy of love. It is a means of meeting. God's words to Moses, "Thou canst not see my face: for there shall no man see me and live,"[23] indicate that a full-on encounter would not work. The becoming as we are is a veiling that makes friendship possible. A master of the keyboard does not tell a little child picking out her first notes on the piano that her efforts are nothing; a gracious guest skilled in cuisine eats without comment the mediocre fare his well-meaning host sets before him; a sharp-witted but loving conversationalist holds back the clever but devastating riposte. We know how to put limits on what we say out of love: God in His Word is the same. Jesus as a baby is wrapped in swaddling clothes; the Lord is with us as a prisoner of the tabernacle as, more terribly, he was a prisoner when He was condemned to death. That limitation is accepted by God.

---

20 Cf Mt 16:18.   21 Ru 1:16.
22 In a commentary on Isaiah in *A Word in Season: Advent to Christmastide* (Petersham, MA: Saint Bede's Publications, 1981).   23 Ex 33:10.

This is a perfection in God, just as the pianist, cook or conversationalist have something extra in the holding of their tongues: not more skill, but more love. If it is a weakness not to show their superiority, it is a weakness in the sense St Paul is indicating when he writes, "We are glad, when we are weak and ye are strong."[24] Love could be considered as a weakness, but it partakes of "the weakness of God" which, as St Paul also said, is "stronger than men."[25] We can also think about God's acceptance of limitation in a metaphysical way, even if this is not as obvious as the human analogy. The infinite can be given something by the finite. Limitation adds something to unlimitedness. If you think about an infinite series of numbers you come to a halt when you try to imagine whether the final number is odd or even because of course if it is odd there could be an even one after it and vice versa. So in truth the infinite is an order of reality different from that of the finite and if there is this difference, then the finite adds something to the infinite, the limited adds something to the unlimited: particularity. That is what the presence of the Lord in His earthly life and in the Blessed Sacrament is doing: it is adding something. God comes to us as a particular person and in a particular way. This is a comfort. To compare the sublime to the mundane: however efficient a company's online dealings are, it really helps if there is someone you can talk to if things go wrong. This is a plus, not a failure to construct the perfect algorithm. Pursuing this line of thought, we can say God is not limited by His unlimitedness or we can say with Nicholas of Cusa that God is the coincidence of opposites, the infinite and the finite.[26] God transcends the infinite by accepting limitation. He lives in eternity in which the limitations — essentially separations — of time and space are absent. Nonetheless He accepts these limitations with the concomitant loss and sorrow of separation in order to walk among us.

24 2 Cor 13:9.   25 1 Cor 1:25.
26 *Nicholas of Cusa, Selected Spiritual Writings*, trans. and intro. H. Lawrence Bond (New York, Mahwah, 1979), 46.

The gospels show us in simple human terms what the Incarnation involves. This is well-known territory. It involves Jesus accepting the limitations of our human condition, so He is hungry, He is tired, He is thirsty. He has a need for friends, so He weeps when His friend Lazarus, whom He loves, dies.[27] When He is in the Garden of Gethsemane He says to Peter, James and John, "Tarry ye (μείνατε/*meinate*) here, and watch with me."[28] He has a human need for abiding friendship. Although they fall asleep, they are there and that means something to Him, that gives something to Him. What is going on here — in the Incarnation — is that Our Lord is putting Himself in a position where He relates to people. There is the possibility of reciprocity, of His receiving as well as giving, of love and friendship. As when He walked the earth, so in His presence in the Blessed Sacrament, Our Lord is wanting friendship. Gospel texts about His earthly life guide us in reflection on His life in the Sacrament. For example, He says to the Samaritan woman, "Give me to drink."[29] She gives Him water from Jacob's well and He tells her that she could have asked Him and He would have given her "living water" such that "whosoever drinketh of this water shall never thirst" for it "shall be in him a well of water springing up to everlasting life."[30] That water is the Holy Spirit, the Spirit of love, which He has to give in return for the water that He is given. So He invites a relationship with us by putting Himself in a position in which He can truly receive from us. In that relationship He can give a return, which is the gift of the Spirit of love, in which giving and receiving, loving and knowing are but one. He wants to give that to us and that is why He is present to us in the Blessed Sacrament.

In order to enter into that friendship with us, He has to be vulnerable. That is the law of any real human interaction, that it is not just one side that gives and one side that receives: it is reciprocal. Imagine that you take to a café someone who without good reason absolutely refuses any drink or food: that would be

27 Jn 11:35.   28 Mt 26:38.   29 Jn 4:7.   30 Jn 4:10–14.

the end of companionship, in the literal and probably also the metaphorical sense of the word. It would be impossible to relate in a hospitable way to such a person. Our Lord comes to us therefore in His vulnerability. He is tender, in two senses of the word: susceptible to pain (He can be rejected) and compassionate (He shows us tender mercy). In the Blessed Sacrament His tender vulnerability is prolonged: He waits for someone who may never come, offering friendship that may not be accepted. In the movie *Slumdog Millionaire* the main character makes contact with the girl he loves by calling her during a television game show. He tells her that he will be waiting for her at the Chhatrapati Shivaji Terminus train station in Mumbai at the same time every day. He just goes on turning up there till she comes. Yet he has no guarantee that she will. He remains there, vulnerable to her rejection every day. The Lord in the Blessed Sacrament enters into such a vulnerability: that of being there for us in a way which we can ignore, the vulnerability of being able to receive from us that which we are able to deny giving, a true human vulnerability. At the same time there is that divine gift that He wants to offer us through His presence.

That alerts us to a second kind of vulnerability in love. We can be vulnerable in love to rejection by somebody refusing the love we have to offer—whether that sung of in courtly love poetry or simply the offer of friendship—but there is another kind of vulnerability that love entails. Perhaps that is at its clearest with the love of a parent for a child, but any love knows this vulnerability. That is the vulnerability of suffering because the person loved suffers and it is not possible to do anything about it. Such is the suffering of the Blessed Virgin at the foot of the cross. Either of these vulnerabilities can in a human sense be partly overcome through a heroic love. For example, in Dickens' *A Tale of Two Cities*, Sidney Carton loves a woman who loves another man, one who looks very like him. When the latter is condemned to execution he heroically swaps clothes with this other and is killed instead of him so that the woman he loves can have the happiness of sharing her life with the man she loves. That is a true love, truly accepted and truly beneficial. It is also possible for a love to survive a terrible thing happening to the one loved. Even if the beloved dies there can be the consolation of the bond of love never having been broken. Terrible as the grief may be, there is a softening of it, the sweetness of knowing that a reciprocal love remained until the end, to say nothing of the heavenly reunion of which faith speaks.

For Our Lord it is different, for He alone can give the Spirit that heals the heart and so a rejection of Him involves a failure in the rescuing of the one He loves—that is, each of us—from what threatens us. This is not just an ordinary death: it is what the Book of Revelation calls "the second death,"[31] an eternal death. It is a double blow: He is not accepted and the one He loves is not healed. That double vulnerability is truly and really present in His person in the Blessed Sacrament: He can be ignored and stopped from healing us.

The thirst of the Lord when He is at the well with the Samaritan woman anticipates His cry from the cross, "I thirst."[32] St Teresa of Calcutta has this citation from the gospel in the tabernacles in her congregation of Missionaries of the Divine Charity. It is interpreted to mean that thirst for the reciprocity of love from all those the Lord loves, that is everybody. It is a thirst for the acceptance of His gift of healing. That is the ultimate vulnerability. God is omnipotent as we say in the creed but God is also the coincidence of opposites, so God is the most vulnerable as well as the most powerful. He transcends omnipotence, choosing to be vulnerable for the sake of love. That vulnerable presence is with us in the Blessed Sacrament. Our Lord suffers as He suffered on the cross because He is not accepted and He is not allowed to heal. The suffering is ongoing. The physical agony of the cross is an instantiation of that deeper pain of not being accepted and allowed to care for the one who is loved. The Lord's suffering

31 Rv 2:11.   32 Jn 19:28.

presence remains. There is a tendency for us to think of care in systemic terms: our society is organized so that care is offered by the state or an organization. We do not go to see a medical specialist and say, "I thought I would spend some time with you because you would like it." It doesn't work like that. The system has been made impersonal to try to get beyond human frailty and the giving of personal favors. God's love is not like that; it is more like a mother's love. God has never given up on human frailty. He Himself becomes frail, sharing our frailty so that we can make that gift to Him of a personal presence for which He longs.

The Sacred Heart

There is of course another aspect to the Lord's presence: his victory, His triumph at Easter, that triumph over rejection and refusal when "He came unto his own, and his own received him not,"[33] and He was excluded from His society and killed. He rises from the dead through divine power. Both the vulnerability and the victory are truly present in the Blessed Sacrament. This presence is not just something like replaying home movies of His earthly life, a simple memory: it is a real ongoing presence of His awesome personal love both vulnerable and victorious. We can say quite simply that here in the Sacrament we have the Sacred Heart of Jesus, that love through which all things were made and without which nothing was made that was made.[34]

This is explicit in an extraordinary book that records words from the Lord and His Mother received in his heart by an anonymous Benedictine monk and priest. Here are some of them:

> Little by little I will lead you into the silence of unitive love . . . I will teach you to imitate John, My beloved disciple, by resting your head — so full of thoughts and cares and fears and words — upon My Most Sacred Heart. There you will learn to find peace and perfect

33 Jn 1:11.   34 Cf Jn 1:3.

happiness in listening only to the steady rhythm of My Heart, which beats with love for you and for all priests. It is not the length of these moments that matters but, rather, the intensity of divine love that fills them.[35]

That love from the Sacred Heart is present for all, not just priests, inviting a response, a response of the heart. *Cor ad cor loquitur* ("heart speaks to heart") — words that St John Henry Newman took as his motto. Responding to the vulnerable personal presence of the Lord with an adoring heart is the business of adoration, whether the Blessed Sacrament is exposed or in the tabernacle. "Adoration" can appropriately mean simply an intense love or it can be interpreted etymologically (from the Latin *orare*, to pray, and *ad*, to) as praying to the Lord. However that prayer is not going to establish a union of hearts if it is simply a wish list or a series of bullet points for the Lord of heaven and earth to attend to, points needing attention from the meeting rather than a meeting of hearts. This is not to say that the Lord is not interested in what troubles us — quite the contrary. The Lord wants to make a meeting of hearts happen — our hearts meeting His with whatever is in them, including (and this is important) all of the sinfulness of our hearts (for "The heart is deceitful above all things and desperately wicked"),[36] all of our worries and our concerns; the Lord wants us to respond to St Peter's exhortation concerning "casting all your care upon him."[37] We are invited to a confidence and trust that He will take care of what troubles us. It is simply a matter of presence, that presence He asked of Peter, James and John in the Garden of Gethsemane, a presence of friendship. He invites this, vulnerable to its refusal but wanting to heal through its acceptance. We can make a return to the Lord through simple silent presence to His love, readiness to receive that love. He, for His part, is present to us, as is abundantly

---

35   *In Sinu Iesu: When Heart Speaks to Heart — The Journal of a Priest at Prayer* (Brooklyn: Angelico Press, 2016), 109.   36   Jer 17:9.   37   1 Pt 5:7.

clear from these words from the book quoted above:

> I am absorbed by your presence before Me. Does it
> shock you that I should say such a thing? But I am
> absorbed by you: My eyes rest upon you; My Heart
> is all yours; I am listening intently to you; and all my
> attention is focused on you when you come seeking
> Me. Believe that I am totally absorbed by you, and
> soon you will be totally absorbed by Me. I speak here
> using human terms, using the language of friendship,
> of affection, of love. I am present here in all the sen-
> sitivity and tenderness of My humanity. I am here
> offering you My friendship, ready to spend as much
> time with you as you are ready to spend with me.[38]

As well as praying in front of the Blessed Sacrament, we can
know something of the mystery of His presence through — to
come back to the Incarnation and Mary — the rosary. Pope St
John Paul II gave us the luminous mysteries of the rosary and
the fifth luminous mystery is that of the institution of the Eucharist: the gift of the Lord Himself in all of His humanity and in
all of His divinity to us till the end of time. Through the rosary,
with Mary, we can contemplate that ever-presence, and in contemplation enter into friendship. We can hear her words, "They
have no wine,"[39] bringing before Him our lack of conviviality,
our need for His redeeming Blood, our need for His friendship.

His Service and Ours

In that friendship Jesus heals us. The account of the Last
Supper in St John's gospel shows us how. "He riseth from supper, and laid aside his garments; and took a towel, and girded
himself."[40] The towel is the human flesh of His incarnation. He
leaves the eternal feast of heaven, and, as John Milton put it:

---

38 *In Sinu Iesu*, 247.   39 Jn 2:3.   40 Jn 13:4.

> That glorious form, that light insufferable,
> And that far-beaming blaze of majesty,
> Wherewith he wont at heaven's high council-table,
> To sit the midst of trinal unity,
> He laid aside; and here with us to be,
> Forsook the courts of everlasting day,
> And chose with us a darksome house of mortal clay.[41]

The poet echoes the words cited above from Scripture — "laid aside" — in the fifth line and in the simplicity of the language of this line, relative to what precedes it, expresses the simplicity of the human life with which He girds Himself. "After that he poureth water into a bason, and began to wash the disciples' feet, and to wipe them with the towel wherewith he was girded."[42] As with the spirit-troubling dream of King Nebuchadnezzar of a "great image" with feet partly of clay,[43] the feet of the disciples symbolize their frailty. When Peter says, "Thou shalt never wash my feet,"[44] he is denying this frailty. That denial anticipates Peter's denial of his Master.[45] Denying his own frailty, Peter denies his need of the Divine Physician, who came "not to call the righteous, but sinners";[46] denying that need and not yet understanding that God's strength "is made perfect in weakness,"[47] Peter acts only in his own strength. That is not enough to save him from fearfully denying the Master he loves.

Peter is all of us who follow Christ. We need the washing of our feet, the healing of our frailty. The Lord's words to Peter, "If I wash thee not, thou hast no part with me,"[48] are addressed to us also. We need healing, cleansing friendship with the Lord to be able to walk in His way as Peter went on to do. That is found in a heart-to-heart with Him in the Blessed Sacrament and in the Sacrament of Reconciliation. Yet, as well as being

---

41 "On the Morning of Christ's Nativity," stanza 2, in *Milton: Complete Shorter Poems*, 101.

42 Jn 13:5.   43 Dn 2:31–45.   44 Jn 13:8.   45 Jn 18:17, 25, 27.

46 Mk 2:17.   47 2 Cor 12:9.   48 Jn 13:8.

insufficiently aware of our frailty as Peter initially was, it is possible to be too overcome by the sense of it. This is beautifully understood in this poem by George Herbert:

> Love bade me welcome: yet my soul drew back,
>   Guiltie of dust and sinne.
> But quick-ey'd Love, observing me grow slack
>   From my first entrance in,
> Drew nearer to me, sweetly questioning,
>   If I lack'd any thing.
>
> A guest, I answer'd, worthy to be here:
>   Love said, You shall be he.
> I the unkinde, ungratefull? Ah my deare,
>   I cannot look on thee.
> Love took my hand, and smiling did reply,
>   Who made the eyes but I?
>
> Truth Lord, but I have marr'd them: let my shame
>   Go where it doth deserve.
> And know you not, sayes Love, who bore the blame?
>   My deare, then I will serve.
> You must sit downe, sayes Love, and taste my meat:
>   So I did sit and eat.[49]

The poem is simply called "Love" and it alerts us to the infinite delicacy of divine love. There is an implicit pun in it on the word "host." The first stanza describes the kind attention of a perfect host welcoming the speaker to a meal; the final stanza points to the host actually being that meal ("taste my meat"). He is the consecrated host in the Eucharist. The supremely gentle love shown by the one who welcomes the guest is also the absolutely unassuming love of the Lord in the Blessed Sacrament. He is a host who cleanses His guest,

---

49 *The Metaphysical Poets*, 142.

as He washed Peter's feet. "You shall be he" means "You will be made worthy" by the redeeming offering of the Body and Blood of the Lord. The poet nonetheless averts his gaze. He gets a response that is full of meaning: "Love took my hand, and smiling did reply, / Who made the eyes but I?" Love makes us; makes our eyes; makes the "I" of each of us. Each "I" is the instantiation of "I AM THAT I AM."[50] He is in our looking; His eye is the source of knowing; His "Spirit of truth," [51] sweet Healer of our gaze, enables us to look even towards Him. Even this assurance does not overcome the poet's shame. He wants his shame to "Go where it doth deserve." The implication of the last word is that it is not worthy even of serving, still less of being served. The Lord of love's acceptance of blame finally persuades him to serve, but He wants to give him still more. He wants to fulfill that saying in the Scripture, "He shall gird himself, and make them sit down to meat, and will come forth and serve them."[52] The simplicity of the monosyllabic final line shows the poet finally accepting that he is a loved child.

The Eucharist is truly a love feast. It gives healing from our shame. When I first said Mass as a priest, I was struck by how sinner-friendly it is. It assumes we are unworthy, as in what all say before communion, "Lord, I am not worthy that you should enter under my roof, but only say the word and my soul shall be healed," but also in the private prayers of the priest, as in the prayer he says as his fingers are washed after offering the gifts: "Wash me, O Lord, from my iniquity and cleanse me from my sin." The love of this feast however extends beyond welcoming the individual with healing from shame. It is the radiant love of the heavenly banquet. It is communion with God, which establishes communion with every other human person. That is true of both the living and the dead. The latter is poetically realized by David Jones in reflection upon the Roman Canon of the Mass:

---

50 Ex 3:14.   51 Jn 14:17.   52 Lk 12:37.

Upon all fore-times.
From before time
his perpetual light
Shines upon them.
Upon all at once
upon each one
whom he invites, bids, us to recall
when we make the recalling of him
daily, at the Stone.
When the offerant
Our *servos*, so theirs whose life is changed
not taken away
is directed to say
Memento etiam.[53]

"The Stone" is the altar at which the Mass is offered, indicating both the stone in the altar (which symbolizes Christ) and, by its solidity, the eternal quality of the sacrifice. All times before are subsumed in the making present of the eternal, the light of which shines upon each of the departed souls, whose life is changed not ended. The priest says "*Memento etiam*" — "remember also" these people. In the divine love there is no separation from them.

To be fully healed, however, we need to reach out healing hands to others and realize the communion with them given in the Mass. Eucharistic life is grateful, loving service. The Lord, referring to His service of His disciples by washing their feet, says, "Ye should do as I have done to you."[54] Having received the word of pardon and healing, we need to "carry this message" as in the twelfth Alcoholics Anonymous step. It is in lifting burdens, giving freedom, feeding the hungry, bringing into our house "the poor that are cast out," clothing the naked and hiding not ourselves from our "own flesh" that we hear the Lord saying, "Then

---

53 "Rite and Fore-time" in David Jones, *The Anathemata: Fragments of an Attempted Writing* (London: Faber & Faber, 1952), 81.   54 Jn 13:15.

shall thy light break forth as the morning, and thy health shall spring forth speedily."[55] Friendship is watching with the Lord as He prays on that Thursday evening, "Not as I will, but as thou wilt";[56] it is also walking with Him as He goes about "doing good and healing."[57] Abiding in that friendship we find healing, so that—like Peter, like Our Lord Himself—we can be a rock for others. We do that in a very particular way when we make promises: they are in a sense the eternal made present in time, offering stability amid its flux. Marriage vows explicitly promise the fidelity of the spouses to each other whatever changes may come. Religious vows express fidelity to God. Both these kinds of vows are a participation in the eternal fidelity of God. Abiding in Him we can offer the tenderness of love. He, our rock, shows us the ultimate tenderness. The next chapter considers this.

---

55 Is 58:6–8.   56 Mt 26:38–39.   57 Acts 10:38.

by the cross of Jesus

FRIDAY, THE COST OF LOVE

Now there stood by the cross of Jesus his mother,
and his mother's sister, Mary the wife of Cleophas,
and Mary Magdalene.[1]

The Lord's Staying

Our Lord's abiding with us, His enduring presence, is the gift
of His abiding on the cross and enduring His passion and death.
His presence comes from this sacrifice. This sacred presence is
invoked in the words of the hymn:

Hold Thou Thy cross before my closing eyes;
Shine through the gloom and point me to the skies;
Heav'n's morning breaks, and earth's vain shadows flee;
In life, in death, O Lord, abide with me.[2]

His passion and death are an accompanying of us as we
approach our transition from time to eternity and in all our
difficulties and sorrows. His staying in His suffering is an invitation to us to stay with Him in all our difficulties and sorrows,
staying in His innocent gentleness. He "suffered for us, leaving
us an example, that ye should follow his steps: Who did no
sin, neither was guile found in his mouth: Who when he was
reviled, reviled not again; when he suffered, he threatened not
but committed himself to him that judgeth righteously; who
his own self bare our sins in his body on the tree, that we being

1 Jn 19:25.   2 Hymn text by Henry Francis Lyte.

dead to sins, should live unto righteousness: by whose stripes you were healed."[3] His endurance is an invitation to our endurance in faith: faith that He is with us and faith that the outcome is joyful. So we are given the exhortation: "let us run with patience the race that is set before us, looking unto Jesus the author and finisher of our faith; who for the joy that was set before him endured the cross, despising the shame."[4] These words had a special importance for me when I had a diagnosis of a potentially lethal cancer; I pondered them in a hospital chapel and was encouraged to reflect that the Lord faced His cross for the sake of joy. That was, and is, an invitation to share in His endurance and so in His joy. Essentially, that is the joy of love: love of the Father, whose will is being accepted and love of those for whom sacrifice is offered. It is the joy of heaven, which ever expands as it knows others knowing too this joy of love.

The Glory of Love

Friday is the day to remember Good Friday, good because of the love and its joy. Anciently it was a day associated with love. In Old English Friday is *frigedæg* meaning "Frigga's day." Frigga (meaning "beloved") is also known as Freya and is the goddess of married love.[5] She is the wife of Odin, the leader of the gods, and in one recounting she can often be found weeping tears of red gold when he is away on long journeys.[6] Such is love: red for the blood of the heart, gold for its costliness. Married love is promised "till death do us part" and reflects the love of Christ for his own "unto the end"[7] and "the great mystery" of the relationship of "Christ and the church."[8] Friday is the day of love. Frigga (or Freya) is identified with Venus whose name is remembered in the French and Italian words for Friday,

---

3 1 Pt 2:21–24.   4 Heb 12:1–2.

5 https://www.etymonline.com/word/Friday#etymonline_v_14178 https://www.etymonline.com/word/Frigg?ref=etymonline_crossreference

6 https://norse-mythology.org/gods-and-creatures/the-aesir-gods-and-goddesses/frigg/   7 Jn 13:1.   8 Eph 5:32.

Vendredi and *Venerdì*. She is known by the Greeks as Aphrodite and by the Babylonians as Ishtar, goddess of love and beauty. Love is beautiful, nowhere so much as on Calvary where in the coincidence of opposites, which is only possible in God, it is shown by the One of whom it was said, "he hath no form nor comeliness; and when we shall see him, there is no beauty that we should desire him."[9] Friday is the day of beautiful love: the ancient and Christian traditions coincide in its name.[10] Friday remembers the goodness of love, spousal and divine, above all manifest on the cross. "Greater love hath no man than this."[11]

It is a love that comes from beyond the loss of everything in this world. In that loss it is broken open so as to have a universal reach. This is given expression in Leonard Cohen's song *Heart with No Companion*:

> Now I greet you from the other side
> Of sorrow and despair
> With a love so vast and shattered
> It will reach you everywhere
>
> And I sing this for the captain
> Whose ship has not been built
> For the mother in confusion
> Her cradle still unfilled
>
> For the heart with no companion
> For the soul without a king
> For the prima ballerina
> Who cannot dance to anything
>
> Through the days of shame that are coming
> Through the nights of wild distress
> Though your promise count for nothing
> You must keep it nonetheless

9 Is 53:2.   10 Cf Held, *Rhythms of the Week*, 66.   11 Jn 15:13.

You must keep it for the captain
Whose ship has not been built
For the mother in confusion
Her cradle still unfilled

For the heart with no companion
For the soul without a king
For the prima ballerina
Who cannot dance to anything

This love is a love for those without, "the poor in spirit."[12] The dispossessed, in the midst of whom is "the heart with no companion," are its recipients. We are open to this love when we acknowledge our powerlessness. It challenges us to be as abidingly faithful to it as was the Lord Jesus. In worldly terms our promise of such fidelity may "count for nothing" but we "must keep it nonetheless." Love is in the intention of the heart rather than in practical accomplishment. We must keep it for the dispossessed through "the days of shame" and "the nights of wild distress" even though it involves for us the loss of all possession in this world. That is in truth no more than facing reality, for we have no abiding possessions in this world.

The cost of entering into and radiating this love is simply the loss of illusion. This is what St John of the Cross calls "complete nakedness and freedom of spirit."[13] It is no longer relying on anything we can possess either through sense or thought. It is pure faith in God's love and, as the Saint writes, "There is no advancing in faith without the closing of one's eyes to everything pertaining to the senses and to clear particular knowledge."[14] T.S. Eliot borrowed the saint's words to give poetic expression to this way of denudation:

---

12 Mt 5:3.   13 *Collected Works of St. John of the Cross*, 68.
14 "The Ascent of Mount Carmel," Ch 16, *Collected Works of St. John of the Cross*, 154.

> In order to possess what you do not possess
>   You must go by the way of dispossession.
> In order to arrive at what you are not
>   You must go through the way in which you are not.
> And what you do not know is the only thing you know
> And what you own is what you do not own
> And where you are is where you are not.[15]

That which is to be no longer possessed or owned is that which belongs to this passing world. Our true being is not seen as such in the terms of this world, nor is true knowing or our true home. That is because they all belong to eternity, not to what passes. Jesus exemplifies abiding in eternity by giving up on the cross all that passes. He helps us to abide in eternity but of course there is pain in reaching this truly healthy life because we are invested in, and have invested in, what passes. He is our surgeon-in-chief. And:

> The wounded surgeon plies the steel
> That questions the distempered part;
> Beneath the bleeding hands we feel
> The sharp compassion of the healer's art
> Resolving the enigma of the fever chart.

To abide truly we need to feel uncomfortable with being settled in what passes:

> Our only health is the disease
> If we obey the dying nurse
> Whose constant care is not to please
> But to remind of our, and Adam's, curse,
> And that, to be restored, our sickness must grow worse.

15 T. S. Eliot, "Four Quartets" in *Collected Poems, 1909–1962* (London: Faber and Faber, 1963), 201. The words of St John of the Cross referenced in the poem come from his diagram of the ascent of Mount Carmel.

We can only be nourished by a sharing in that unyielding separation from the passing that Jesus endures on the cross. Our tendency is to say that we are all right as we are, yet some obscure instinct tells us that this separation is beneficent and good:

> The dripping blood our only drink,
> The bloody flesh our only food
> In spite of which we like to think
> That we are sound, substantial flesh and blood —
> Again, in spite of that, we call this Friday good.[16]

The sharing in the vast and shattered love that comes from the cross, that is the pain of separation from the ephemeral that this love entails, is our glory, of which St Paul wrote, "I reckon that the sufferings of this present time are not worthy to be compared with the glory that shall be revealed in us."[17] The Christian calling is to see in this pain a lifting up, as Christ was "lifted up" on the cross.[18] Our pain is our glory, not because of the suffering but because of the love, as the cross is the glory of the Lord because of His love. Our participation in the Lord's cross is a participation in His glory, the latter incomparably greater than the former. Hence St Paul says, "God forbid that I should glory, save in the cross of our Lord Jesus Christ"[19] and includes in that his own "infirmities."[20] This both identifies him with the suffering Lord and lays open his need of the Savior. When it is a pain to do things for others, when others are a pain, when our love for another brings us pain, staying with the Lord Jesus in His suffering and concomitant glory is the way to be happy. "We count them happy which endure,"[21] says St James.

The Joy of Endurance

It all pivots on acceptance. We endure by accepting with a good will what we have been sent. We have a choice about how

---

16 *Collected Poems*, 201–2.   17 Rom 8:18.   18 Jn 12:32.
19 Gal 12:14.   20 2 Cor 12:9.   21 Ja 5:11.

we take whatever it is that we have been sent. This is brought out in Edith Eger's remarkable memoir of how she survived Auschwitz and the horrors of the holocaust, *The Choice.* In her true story people's choices make all the difference: the choice "to pay attention to what we've lost or to what we still have"; the choice of the liberating soldier to resist the temptation to rape her in her vulnerable state; her choice to stand "on the site of Hitler's former home and forgive him." We always have the freedom to choose our attitude, and so "each moment is a choice."[22] These choices make us who we are: tender people or hard people. One way or another we all know the heat of affliction, but it can cook us different ways: like a potato that becomes soft in the center the more it is baked or like an egg that becomes hard in the center the more it is boiled. How we accept what happens to us determines which way it is. We do not have to undertake this acceptance alone. It has in one sense even been done for us; certainly, the grace of acceptance has been won for us.

The place of this acceptance and this victory is the Garden of Gethsemane where Jesus prayed, "not my will, but thine be done"[23] and "being in agony he prayed more earnestly."[24] We participate in that acceptance when we watch on Holy Thursday but also every time we pray, "thy will be done" in the "Our Father." It is a prayer of mutual indwelling. Jesus had "Peter and James and John" with Him in the garden where he was "very heavy"[25] but they fell asleep.[26] Our watching with Him as He is present in the Blessed Sacrament gives Him human consolation. His dwelling in us as we face our trials and troubles gives us a share in His divine joy. As St Thérèse remarkably observed: "Our Lord in the Garden of Olives enjoyed all the delights of the Trinity, and nevertheless his agony was not the less cruel on account of it. It is a mystery, but I assure you that I understand

---

22 Edith Eger, *The Choice* (London: Penguin Random House, 2017), 50, 98, 280, 204.

23 Lk 22:42.   24 Lk 22:44.   25 Mk 14:33.   26 Mk 14:37.

something of it through what I experience myself."[27] It is not simply that suffering endured for Christ's sake leads to the joy of heaven: intuitively, maybe with some obscurity and certainly without any analgesic effect, that joy can be known in time, as eternity severs in the present moment the bonding together of grief from the past and fear of the future. Such joy sources the steadfastness of the martyrs. Faith does not abolish pain, but through it we are rooted and abide in eternal joy, already in spirit in the hour of which the Lord speaks when He says, "Your sorrow shall be turned into joy... and your heart shall rejoice, and your joy no man taketh from you."[28]

The place of endurance, where joy is seeded, is "by the cross of Jesus" where "there stood... his mother, and his mother's sister, Mary the wife of Cleophas, and Mary Magdalene."[29] Here we witness, and are witnesses to, the ultimate tenderness, both in the sense of wounds that are sore to the touch and in the sense of compassionate love. We see the Lord as a "tender plant... a man of sorrows, and acquainted with grief"[30] who was "wounded for our transgressions... bruised for our iniquities."[31] Here is tenderness in the sense of woundedness. What follows is tenderness in the sense of compassion: "He shall see of the travail of his soul, and shall be satisfied; by his knowledge shall my righteous servant justify many; for he shall bear their iniquities."[32] That justifying knowledge is redeeming love. Essentially it is connection (knowledge and love, which are the same thing in God) established with the outcast soul in the place of his or her casting out. It is therefore forgiveness, which is prayed for explicitly for those who do the crucifying in the awesome words, "Father forgive them; for they know not what they do"[33] and implicitly for all of us complicit with evil whose net brings Him to this place. It is a mercy powerful enough to draw all to Him,[34] the most sinful to the All-Holy. The cross is the coincidence of opposites:

27 St Thérèse, *J'entre dans la Vie: Derniers entretiens* (Paris: Le Cerf, 1983), 58.
28 Jn 16:20, 22.   29 Jn 19:25.   30 Is 53:2–3.   31 Is 53:5.
32 Is 53:11.   33 Lk 23:34.   34 Cf Jn 12:32.

the indivisible unity of God and the tearing away from God of sin; the human and divine; the horizontal and the vertical. It is love to the end: the still point of the turning world, the ultimate abiding, and the ultimate tenderness.

Suffering as a Tenderness of God

It is a tenderness of God to let us share that tenderness. This is true in the relatively obvious sense of His enabling us to forgive by giving us forgiveness, as in the parable of the servant forgiven a great debt and expected by his master to forgive a fellow servant a small debt.[35] God's compassion for us makes it possible for us to be compassionate to others, and the giving of that possibility is an aspect of His compassion. Yet, more counter-intuitively, it can also be claimed that it is a tenderness of God to give us the opportunity to be tender in the double sense of Christ's tenderness on the cross: the tenderness of wounds and of compassion. It is the tenderness of allowing us to share in the joy of His loving by uniting our own sufferings to His sacrifice. He suffers with us, and in us: we are never alone in our suffering. The balm of His presence transforms such suffering from something that isolates to something that unites. Suffering takes us deeper into the humanity that we share with others. With Christ in whom and through whom everyone is loved we find communion precisely where, according to worldly wisdom, it is least expected. Peace "not as the world giveth"[36] flows from us to others when we offer our suffering in union with Christ. The acceptance of our woes and the making a gift of our pains in that union bring grace to them. This is so because there is never any final injustice; if we suffer loss, that loss is divinely made good. If this is not done horizontally in terms of worldly prosperity (as often proclaimed in the Old Testament, as for example when "the LORD gave Job twice as much as he had before")[37] then it is done vertically in spiritual blessing which can be offered for others. In the latter case the

35 Mt 18:23–35.   36 Jn 14:27.   37 Jb 42:10.

good realized is eternal. The evil suffered on the worldly level becomes a good on the level of eternity. It is as though, to compare the great with the small, an injustice suffered by a passenger on an economy class flight from a steward results in her being upgraded by the captain to business class. Of course airlines are not always run with perfect justice, but it is an article of Christian faith that God is just and that He is Lord of heaven and earth.

The idea of suffering turning people into fountains of compassion, love and peace perhaps needs a little more explanation, as it is both natural and common for us to feel more inclined to help others when we are not troubled and less so inclined when troubles make us grumpy. The starting point is that explained above, that justice is always operative so that if we do not get it on a material level we do get it in spiritual benefits. It does need to be emphasized that stuff needs to be accepted in the right spirit: if we meet our trouble with angry unbelief, wanting, as it were, to get our own back on God for letting this happen to us, then we are going to be less receptive to spiritual benefit than if we, to use a traditional pious phrase, "offer it up." However, troubles of any kind can be offered up, even the trouble of discovering that we are grumpy people not instinctively reaching out with kindness to those who bother us! So why does starting this practice not always swiftly turn someone into a fountain of compassion? Pursuing the water metaphor gives an indication. If water is spiritual benefit given to one offering things up then it may not become a fountain until the dry and parched land in which it is flowing has quenched its thirst. The water level will need to reach a certain height before a fountain bubbles up from the ground. To put it in old-fashioned, but perfectly valid, terms, we need to offer up what happens to us for our sins before we are holy enough to overflow with compassion, love and peace. When the spiritual beneficence has flooded the once dry territory of our souls then there will be lakes of it from which others too can draw refreshment. Notice that the critical thing is not how well we manage to grit our teeth and bear what is happening, or even how extensive are the depredations that affect our life: the critical thing is *faith*. That is: believing that God truly has the whole world in his care and that all things indeed "work together for good to them that love God"[38] and that inwardly and unseen He is working a mighty blessing for us since "the sufferings of this present time are not worthy to be compared with the glory which shall be revealed in us."[39] This faith changes everything. It is the philosopher's stone, turning the lead of worldly trouble into the gold of heavenly beatitude whose radiance other people can pick up on even in this life.

The saints lived this faith. St Peter lived out the destiny prophesied to him by the Lord: "When thou shalt be old, thou shalt stretch forth thy hands, and another shall gird thee, and carry thee whither thou wouldest not."[40] Peter, who is in a sense every Christian, brings blessing to others by his suffering. Tradition even suggests that, to pursue a perhaps inadequately serious metaphor, he can *give* flight upgrades at the boarding gate for our final departure from this life. St Paul went as far as to write to the Colossians that he rejoiced in his sufferings for them and filled up in his flesh "that which is behind of the afflictions of Christ . . . for his body's sake, which is the church."[41] St Thérèse wrote to her sister Céline about the terrible family affliction of the insanity of their father, "Oh let us not lose the trial that Jesus sends us, it's a gold-mine to exploit, are we going to miss the opportunity?" Truly suffering was to her a special tenderness of God, not something to complain about: she asserted, "Far from complaining to Jesus about the cross he is sending us, I cannot understand the *infinite* love that has led him to treat us this way."[42] To her it was a gift: she received it with the words, "What a privilege Jesus gives us in sending us such a great *sorrow*, ah! ETERNITY will not be too long to thank him."[43] The

---

38 Rom 8:28.   39 Rom 8:18.   40 Jn 21:18.   41 Col 1:24.
42 St Thérèse, *Correspondance générale*, vol 1 (Paris, 1972), letter of Feb. 28, 1890, 459.   43 *Correspondance*, Letter to Céline of Mar. 5, 1889, 463.

privilege consists in having the soul detached from the created: although their affliction was "a great blow" it was "a blow of love."[44] An increase in faith as it is strengthened in its exercise of looking beyond what this world offers to God's loving purpose; an increase of hope in God as the hopelessness of relying on this world only becomes more apparent; an increase in love for God as He is turned to for consolation when there is no other: these are the true and abiding goods — "now abideth faith, hope, charity, these three."[45]

The dynamic is in the ambiguity of the word "tenderness." The wound, tender though it is, opens one up to love that comes from beyond the creation and that love makes one tender in the positive sense of having a heart open to another. There is a similar ambiguity in the word "care." The cares of this life can be seen in a merely negative way or they can be accepted with an awareness that they soften the heart in sympathy for others: some of them can even be chosen as troubles taken to help others. A caring person is a careworn person lit up with love. A third such ambiguous word is "stroke." It is at one and the same time an affliction that affects the brain and a bodily sign of love. Indeed, in the case of a left-brain stroke the relative weakening of the capacity to manipulate things and concepts (the left-brain directs the right hand) can increase the capacity characteristic of the right-brain to look at things as a whole and respond with love. That is to say, to put it simply, that the life of the person so affected becomes less focused on means and more focused on ends. The mental activity associated with getting things done gives way to that associated with more holistic considerations, such as love and God. One indication of this is that the right brain directs the left hand, in which a baby

---

44 *Correspondance*, Letter to Céline of July 14, 1889, 494.
45 1 Cor 13:13. The idea of faith, hope and love growing through suffering is explored at greater length in my book *Paradise on Earth: Exploring a Christian response to suffering* (Stowmarket, Suffolk: Kevin Mayhew, 1993).

is normally held.[46] The ambiguity of the words "tender," "care" and "stroke" reflects an ambiguity in all that happens: there is some good, some possibility of increase of love in the soul, in everything. Evil, which is always parasitic on good, cannot be pure. As Shakespeare wrote: "There is some soul of goodness in things evil, / Would men observingly distill it out."[47] When we do this, "We gather honey from the weed."[48] The "honey" can be a strengthening of our love for God, which the outwardly bad can occasion. The more we are established in that, the more applicable are those words of St Paul, "We know that all things work together for good to them that love God."[49] It is of course not always obvious what the good is or easy to focus on it, but the more we abide in God the more we can take a positive view after the manner of St Thérèse who said, "I always see the good side of things"[50] and, as St Paul enjoins, give "thanks always for all things."[51] That abiding develops a deep seeing.

The Gift of Mary

St John abided and saw. He was the only male follower of the Lord to remain by His cross. In Mel Gibson's film *The Passion of the Christ*, John's still, quiet contemplative gaze seems to express a knowledge of the gift and grace flowing from the horror unfolding. He models abiding for us. It is his special part to be close to the Lord, even when "there is no beauty" and others hide their faces.[52] That closeness properly extends to standing by all who suffer, for He will say, "Insomuch as ye have done it unto one of the least of these my brethren, ye have done it unto me."[53] And in doing that we receive a great gift, for "When Jesus therefore saw his mother, and the disciple standing

---

46 Cf. Iain McGilchrist, *The Master and His Emissary: The Divided Brain and the Making of the Western World* (New Haven: Yale University Press, 2009). This book gives a full account of what is presented here as the merest sketch.

47 *Henry V*, Act 4, Scene 1, lines 4-5.   48 *Henry V*, Act 4, Scene 1, line 11.

49 Rom 8:28.   50 *Thérèse de L'Enfant-Jésus*, 1004.   51 Eph 5:20.

52 Is 53:2–3.   53 Mt 25:40.

by, whom he loveth, he saith unto his mother, Woman, behold thy son! Then saith he to the disciple, Behold thy mother! And from that hour that disciple took her unto his own home."[54] Mary is a great gift because she is the Mother of divine life in us. Through her comes the One who says "I am the resurrection, and the life,"[55] through her comes our heavenly life. She is the one standing by the cross

> Who was God's partner here, and furnish'd thus
> Half of that Sacrifice, which ransom'd us.[56]

She nurtures us. Through her prayer come the graces we need, through her life comes the teaching we need. As a mother teaches her child to belong to society by indicating the appropriate behavior, so she shows us the way of heaven. We go there by the good we do and the evil we suffer, and she shows us how to undertake both. She directs our attention to the Way, saying "Whatsoever he saith unto you, do it."[57] So we are to love the Lord our God with all our heart and all our soul and with all our strength and with all our mind and our neighbor as our self,[58] and pray as He did, "Not my will, but thine, be done,"[59] accepting what is sent to us.

Mary did. She believed the words of the Archangel Gabriel, "With God nothing shall be impossible"[60] and said to the Lord, "Be it unto me according to thy word,"[61] accepting both the destiny prophesized to her—"a sword shall pierce through thy own soul also"[62]—and the promise of the Lord of "joy no man taketh from you."[63] The pain and the joy were implicit in the acceptance. It was a choice of life, both in the sense of not retreating from its demands and so being open to its joy and in the sense of welcoming Him who is "the resurrection and

54 Jn 19:26–27.   55 Jn 11:25.
56 John Donne, "Good Friday, 1613, Riding Westward," in *The Metaphysical Poets*, 87.   57 Jn 2:5.   58 Lk 10:27.   59 Lk 22:42.
60 Lk 2:37–38.   61 Lk 1:38.   62 Lk 2:35.   63 Jn 16:22.

the life."[64] It was a choice of everything that God asked of and offered to her. St Thérèse records in her autobiography a similar choice. As a little child she was offered by an older sister a choice from what was in a basket of bits of cloth and so on, and she said, "I choose everything," taking the basket and everything in it. True to her infant self, she went on to choose every sacrifice the Lord asked of her, everything He wanted.[65] Even on the level of natural psychology, accepting everything in the sense of not wishing away part of one's life because one takes issue with how it has been arranged makes for a happy wholesomeness. On the level of the supernatural, accepting every sacrifice the Lord asks, it makes for an awe-inspiring holiness. Mary embodies that, accepting even the sacrifice of her own Son. We open ourselves to her holiness by praying the rosary, contemplating the events of the Lord's life with her who "kept all these things, and pondered them in her heart."[66] Through this prayer with her we abide in the presence of the Lord.

And as a mother Mary has an infinitely tender heart. In the normal way of things, long before we learn philosophy (if we do), we learn that our mother loves us and that we can go to her in our weakness. Unlike our own mothers, Mary is immaculate and so utterly unfailing in her tenderness. In our seeking to be established in God so we may be tender, she is both our role model and our refuge. God is established in her so she is tender! We can always turn to her, always return to her, always trust her. In this too John is our exemplar. Tradition says that he took her to Ephesus. According to the visions of Blessed Anne Catherine Emmerich, he had a house built for her near the city, where she lived for nine years.[67] On 29th July 1891 an expedition led by a French Lazarist priest, Father Jung, discovered the house.[68] Its

---

64 Jn 11:25.   65 *Thérèse de L'Enfant-Jésus*, 84–85.   66 Lk 2:19.

67 Anne Catherine Emmerich, *The Life of the Virgin Mary* (Brooklyn: Angelico Press, 2018), 279–280.

68 Eugene Poulin, *The Holy Virgin's House: The True Story of Its Discovery*, trans. Ivi Richichi (Instanbul: Arikan Yayinlari, 1999), 70.

position corresponded to what the visionary said, "that from the top of the mountain where the house stands one can see Ephesus from one side, and the sea from the other, the sea being nearer than Ephesus."[69] Father Jung looked and knew:

> Yes, it was the place. To the north-east was Ayasou-louk, the plain of Ephesus, the ruins lying there of the city of Prion like a horse-shoe. To the west and south-west, the sea spread out. Samos was in view with its numerous peaks, looking like islands spread out in the middle of the waves.[70]

On a second expedition, "details one after the other" were found to correspond to the description of the visionary. "The house was divided into two parts by a hearth in the centre" and there was "a place for a narrow door" and a recognizable alcove.[71] After a third expedition, the priest was able to write to his ecclesiastical superior, "The only thing we can say is: 'Here is Mary's House.'"[72] Popes Paul VI and John Paul II came in pilgrimage in the last century to this house where, on a stone altar, St John the Divine celebrated Mass. According to St Irenaeus, who knew St Polycarp who knew St John, it was at Ephesus that the beloved disciple produced the fourth gospel.[73]

We are called to this house filled with divine love, at least in a pilgrimage of the heart, for we are that disciple loved by the Lord and this disciple's gospel is the charter of our inheritance of such love. The essence of who we are as Christians is to receive that love from the Lord: the intimacy as given to John, the Spirit of love as given to the Church, the love of the ever-welcoming Father as given to the prodigal son, the love of the Mother given to all her children. The critically necessary disposition is openness to that love. By what it is it will overflow to others. By what

69 Ibid., 33.   70 Ibid., 34.   71 Ibid., 43–44.   72 Ibid., 51.
73 St Irenaeus, *Against the Heresies*, 3.1,1.

it is, it will engender a love for its Giver. Receiving it, we will be able to respond to the two great commandments to love God and neighbor. We will be able to respond to our vocation, to abide in our home overlooking Ephesus.

The visionary tells us that "Mary had made a kind of way of the cross" behind her house and had marked Stations of the Cross with stones or a tree with a mark on it, evidence of which the French explorers found.[74] Sitting at each one, she would renew in her heart "the mystery of its significance . . . praising the Lord for his love with tears of compassion."[75] With her we can abide with Jesus in His holy suffering, whether that is by meditating on it directly, by joining our suffering to His, or by being with others in their suffering. To stand at the foot of the cross is to abide doubly. It is to abide in the sense of staying there, as did John, Mary, Mary the wife of Cleophas and Mary Magdalene. That is as it were the horizontal element of the cross, enduring over time. And standing at the foot of the cross is also abiding in the eternal, the transcendent. That is the vertical element. Together they form the cross, the intersection of time and eternity, the point where steadfastness in the troubles of this life meets the abiding love of God, where His grace pours into the world. To abide there faithfully is to be in the presence of His eternally abiding fidelity to His mercy. In the cross, the source of redemption, they are one and the same. The cross is where we truly abide in this world. The final chapter looks at what it is to be established in this true abiding and to know at the last the eternal abiding beyond this world.

74 Poulin, *The Holy Virgin's House*, 46.
75 Emmerich, *The Life of the Virgin Mary*, 284.

CHAPTER SEVEN

a white stone

SATURDAY, THE WISDOM OF AGE

*Thou wilt keep him in perfect peace, whose mind
is stayed on thee: because he trusteth in thee.*[1]

Lively Stones

The book of Revelation contains a beautiful promise: "To him
that overcometh will I give of the hidden manna, and will give
him a white stone, and in the stone a new name written, which
no man knoweth saving he that receiveth it."[2] The stone is our
true and deepest self, our true identity, always there. It is the
being we have from God, always there within our existence in
this world but not always animadverted to. It is the rock who is
Christ, who is our true life, yet it is also who we uniquely are.
It is divine life and personal identity. It is nourished by Christ,
the manna hidden within but outwardly received in Holy Communion. It is the culmination of the refusal to stay in what is
passing to allow the victory of the abiding.

This victory is through faith: "For whosoever is born of God
overcometh the world: and this is the victory that overcometh
the world, even our faith."[3] Faith overcomes the tendency to
invest in "things on the earth"[4] as though they offered an abiding
home. Through faith we receive Jesus whom "having not seen"
we love.[5] Receiving Him as "the Son of God"[6] we overcome the
world since we are given "power to become sons of God"[7] on

---

1 Is 26:3.   2 Rv 2:17.   3 1 Jn 5:4.   4 Col 3:2.   5 1 Pt 1:8.
6 1 Jn 5:5.   7 Jn 1:12.

account of the "manner of love the Father has bestowed on us."[8]
A stone symbolizes this overcoming, this filial abiding in the
eternity of God, because it is solid and unchanged. As in the
dream that King Nebuchadnezzar has about a stone breaking "a
great image,"[9] which Daniel interprets, the stone represents the
kingdom set up by "the God of heaven" which "shall stand for
ever,"[10] overcoming the kingdoms of this world represented by
the "great image." A stone is unmoved by wind and by rain; a
soul that has overcome the world does not give way to gusts of
passion nor is it destroyed by tears of grief. It reigns with the
authority of the King of kings. St Peter explains the gift of this
kingly power received through Jesus "to whom coming, as unto
a living stone, disallowed indeed of men, but chosen of God,
and precious, Ye also, as lively stones, are built up a spiritual
house, an holy priesthood, to offer up spiritual sacrifices, accept-
able to God by Jesus Christ."[11] Christ as "a living stone" shows
us what it means to be a mature Christian: a rock for others
because abiding yet with a heart not stone but flesh, stable and
tender, anchored and compassionate. In being rock-like through
our faith in Christ we are following Peter who said, "Thou art
the Christ, the Son of the living God" and was told "Thou art
Peter, and upon this rock I will build my church."[12] The stability
of his maturity is foundational for the Church. It models for us
what it is to be a "lively stone."

The Wisdom of Age

The highest exemplar of Christian maturity, however, is
Mary. Here, from the visionary cited in the previous chapter, is
a description of her in her final years:

> I saw the Blessed Virgin as very full of years, but no
> sign of old age appeared in her except a consuming

8 1 Jn 3:1.   9 Dn 2:31.   10 Dn 2:44.   11 1 Pt 2:4–5.
12 Mt 16:16, 18.

yearning by which she was as it were transfigured. There was an indescribable solemnity about her. I never saw her laugh, though she had a beautiful smile. As she grew older, her face became ever paler and more transparent. She was very thin, but I saw no wrinkles; there was no sign whatever in her of any withering or decay. She was living in the spirit, as it were.[13]

Saturday is Mary's day. It is also the last day of the week, the day of this maturity exemplified by Mary. Mary's privilege of being wrinkle-free may not be granted to us as we grow old, but we may nonetheless be able to say with St Paul, "Though our outward man perish, yet the inward man is renewed day by day."[14] The renewal is the liveliness of the stone, our immortal and unshakeable being. After the manner of Mary's being as it were transfigured by her yearning, we have a kind of transfiguration from our orientation to the life of the resurrection which is apt to Saturday, the day before the day of the resurrection, the day for confidently awaiting the joy of the resurrection. It is the day of those whose old age gives them hope of the imminence of heaven. In Old English Saturday is *sæterdæg*, literally "day of the planet Saturn."[15] This planet is associated with the heaviest metal, lead, and with the solemnity and wisdom of that old age, epitomized by the "indescribable solemnity" of Mary, the fount of wisdom. In ancient Roman tradition the reign of Saturn was called the golden age and he gives his name to the meter in which the oldest Latin poems were written. Saturday is the day for looking back at the week and seeing its gifts and graces; the wisdom of age is to see the gift and grace of life received, to understand it in its golden aspect. This way of seeing is given expression in *Gold Leaves* by G.K. Chesterton:

13 Emmerich, *Life of the Virgin Mary*, 287.   14 2 Cor 4:16.
15 https://www.etymonline.com/word/Saturday#etymonline_v_22771

Lo! I am come to autumn,
When all the leaves are gold;
Grey hairs and golden leaves cry out
The year and I are old.

In youth I sought the prince of men,
Captain in cosmic wars,
Our Titan, even the weeds would show
Defiant, to the stars.

But now a great thing in the street
Seems any human nod,
Where shift in strange democracy
The million masks of God.

In youth I sought the golden flower
Hidden in wood or wold,
But I am come to autumn,
When all the leaves are gold.

The poem is about the gracious acceptance of all that is good. There are two parallel images in the poem: one of plants (golden flower — gold leaves) and one of people (prince of men — all people). They both illustrate the move from concentration on the particular to wider sympathy as one gets older. The youth of the second stanza is seeking a hero, probably a revolutionary leader. This character is described three times, all as objects of the verb "I sought": he is "the prince of men," the "captain in cosmic wars" and "our Titan." The most famous Titan is Prometheus, who aided mankind to rebel against the gods, perhaps represented by "the stars." The young person does not have a Christian vision. He seeks "the golden flower" — the prince / captain / Titan character who would show "even the weeds . . . defiant to the stars." In other words, the revolutionary leader (after the manner of Robespierre or Trotsky) would inspire the common people to rise up and determine their own fate. In the next stanza the speaker has gotten older, realized that the search for a great human hero is futile, and sees that all human beings are in the image of God. "Any human nod" is therefore more than a mere acknowledgement: it is a divine blessing, for people are God's "million masks." The realization of the truth of this is our "autumn,/When all the leaves are gold."

Abiding in the Word

The serenity of a spiritually realized old age comes from abiding in the eternal; it is indeed already living an eternal life. It grows within like a butterfly in a chrysalis, ready to wing its way to empyrean blue when its hour is come, yet already its radiance and peace is perceptible — perhaps in the eyes or the imperturbability of the one who has it. Essentially this abiding in eternal life is a priestly quality, linking earth and heaven, and all Christians share it through their communion with Christ "the high priest for ever after the order of Melchisedec."[16] It is a birth "not of blood, nor of the will of the flesh, nor of the will of man, but of God."[17] This life is like that of the great priest Melchisedec who, "without father, without mother, without descent, having neither beginning of days, nor end of life; but made like unto the Son of God; abideth a priest continually."[18] It finds its joy in God whatever happens on earth, saying with prophet Habbakuk,

> Although the fig tree shall not blossom, neither shall fruit be in the vines; the labour of the olive shall fail, and the fields shall yield no meat; the flock shall be cut off from the fold, and there shall be no herd in the stalls: Yet I will rejoice in the LORD, I will joy in the God of my salvation.[19]

16 Heb 6:20.   17 Jn 1:13.   18 Heb 7:3.   19 Heb 3:17–18,

It is a communion in "the power of an endless life."[20] It is an abiding in the unshakeable word of the Lord. "And this word, Yet once more, signifieth the removing of those things that are shaken, as of things that are made, that those things which cannot be shaken may remain,"[21] comments the writer to the Hebrews about this prophecy in the book of Haggai: "Yet once more I shake not the earth only, but also heaven."[22] All of creation, it follows, is subordinate to this eternal and abiding life. This life is so fundamental that anything that can be changed will be changed if that it is what it takes for it to remain. Our part in its abiding is simply to remain in the grace of God: "Wherefore we receiving a kingdom which cannot be moved, let us have grace, whereby we may serve God acceptably with reverence and Godly fear: For our God is a consuming fire."[23]

The Smoke of Her Burning

This fire of God consumes all that does not abide. Significantly, the very next verse in the letter to the Hebrews reads, "Let brotherly love continue" this last word being μενέτω (*menetō*), cognate with the word for abiding, μένειν (*menein*), that we have been considering in this book. Fraternal love abides for "God is love"[24] and "everyone that loveth is born of God."[25] If we are born of God, we are "heirs of God,"[26] inheritors of His immutability. What is not abiding, that which belongs to the merely mercantile ways of the world rather than to love, all of that passes, "For here we have no continuing (μένουσαν/*menousan*) city."[27] Typologically the doing of deals that replaces love is indicated by the city of Babylon. And the merchants there,

> which were made rich by her, shall stand afar off for
> the fear of her torment, weeping and wailing, And

---

20 Heb 7:16.   21 Heb 12:27.   22 Heb 12:26.   23 Heb 12:28–29.
24 1 Jn 4:8.   25 1 Jn 4:7.   26 Rom 8:17.   27 Heb 13:14.

saying, Alas, alas, that great city, that was clothed in fine linen, and purple, and scarlet, and decked with gold, and precious stones, and pearls! For in one hour so great riches is come to nought. And every ship-master, and all the company in ships, and sailors, and as many as trade by sea, stood afar off, And cried when they saw the smoke of her burning, saying, What city is like unto this great city![28]

This prophecy from the book of Revelation warns all who belong to the worldly nexus that has replaced love of all with a self-interested making mere merchandise of life that they cannot abide the fire of God's final appearance! Since our world is now patterned by economic consideration, and since "ye cannot serve God and mammon,"[29] it is clear enough it cannot last. That is becoming more obvious in our day and the apparent tendency of our world order to dissolve is providential for that reason. God is established and Satan, the prince of this world and the father of lies, angry "because he knoweth that he hath but a short time,"[30] would like to establish this world of flux as a fixed point, which it cannot be.

Harmony in the Whole

The normal view (to pick up again the argument of the first chapter) is represented by Plato, for whom time is the moving image of eternity. What relates to this changing world, what is now considered "science," he calls "opinion" for it changes, unlike the stable and eternal. The notion that what can be established by measurement and calculation about this sublunary world is somehow an absolute is a diabolical lie. Making the foundation of life "evidence based" is the attempt to live from death, for the measured is what is not moving on and the recorded is fixed, like the duchess' portrait on the wall.

28 Rv 18:15–18.   29 Mt 6:24.   30 Rv 12:12.

That is not to say that science as we know it cannot give useful insights, simply that the true absolute transcends what we know through our senses. The error is to suppose that what we know in space and time is a closed system which can be explained in terms of itself. Anything built on this supposition is subject to the fire of the apocalypse as the divine truth subsumes it. We are called to live from the stable, but now largely forgotten, perspective that understands that everything is sustained by the divine, instead of from the aberrant instability of a this-worldly view. We have to lose the life that leads to decay and death because it is rooted in what is passing to find life that is true and eternal because it rests on the rock who is Christ. "All things were made by him"[31] and if they are considered as whole and complete they do not move. Understood as coming from a divine source they are eternally present to that source because it is eternal. They are always what they are; there is no change.

It is when we identify with part of the creation instead of with Him through whom it is made that we are tossed about by mutability, as is captured by these lines from a sonnet:

> Love of the world comes in many forms
> one can love the world from in the world
> and be like a leaf tossed between storms
> or step outside and be like a baby curled[32]

Seen from within time, particular things come and go. There is disturbing change. Seen from eternity, the whole is beautiful and complete. This vision has the trusting peace and innocence of "a baby curled," free from any personal agenda and it sees the harmony that is in the whole. As the poet just cited recognizes, this looking at the whole picture — a goal rather than a starting point — is a loving gaze:

31 Jn 1:3.   32 "Love of the World" by Sam Davidson. Used by permission.

the way to love, I know it not but see
a way to hold the whole world in your heart
it is by stepping out from what you see
not neglecting the whole for the part[33]

It is selfish partiality which leads to pain that seems intolerable: the insistence on one thing rather than another; preferring one's own will to God's. Looking from within the mutable the children of the world ask, with Pilate, "What is truth?"[34] Established in the absolute we bear witness, with Christ, "unto the truth," the truth of the divine unity in which all has its beautiful meaning.[35]

Living from the truth, setting our "affections on things above,"[36] we can love Christ as our King and have the confidence of the prophet: "Thou wilt keep him in perfect peace, whose mind is stayed on thee: because he trusteth in thee."[37] The world cannot give this peace which comes from above and gives us an untroubled and unafraid heart, but Christ promises it: "Peace I leave with you, my peace I give unto you: not as the world giveth, give I unto you. Let not your heart be troubled, neither let it be afraid."[38] In a particular way, it is at the heart of the life of a Benedictine monk, but it is a gift to every Christian. With our eyes fixed on the Lord Christ we know the truth of His words "he that seeth me seeth him that sent me"[39] and are confident that our gaze is settled on the Father almighty, maker of heaven and earth. Such a stable orientation calms sorrow. As a poet put it, "The imaged Word, it is, that holds / Hushed willows anchored in its glow."[40] Weeping the willows may be, but they know a warmth of love that keeps them steady. The admonition of St James, "Stablish your hearts"[41] is an invitation to this peace-giving anchoring in the Eternal. That anchoring, where "neither moth nor rust doth corrupt,"[42] is the only way to a stable heart.

---

33 "Love of the World."   34 Jn 18:38.   35 Jn 18:37.   36 Col 3:2.
37 Is 26:3.   38 Jn 14:27.   39 Jn 13:45.
40 Hart Crane, *Complete Poems*, ed. Brom Weber (Hexham, UK: Bloodaxe Books, 1984), 59.   41 Jas 5:8.   42 Mt 6:20.

Rock-like and Tender

Such a heart can be a rock for another because it is not closed. Its rock-like stability enables it to stay open. In an apparent paradox, it is both solid and melted. God lives in it, and in God is the coincidence of opposites, as Nicholas of Cusa observed.[43] God is both transcendent and immanent; such a heart is both set on what is above and intimately present to those suffering below. In God truth and love coincide; such a heart speaks "the truth in love."[44] Such a heart's staying in the truth makes possible its tender love and vice-versa. The connection between the two is made by St Paul writing to the Thessalonians: "And the Lord make you to increase and abound in love one toward another and toward all men, even as we do toward you: To the end he may stablish your hearts unblameable in holiness before God."[45] In this heart the divine, eternally established and stayed, is united with the human and tender. In it is Christ, true God and true Man. The heart of this heart is His Sacred Heart. The spark of the divine enlightens its spirit with compassion. Stayed like this, the heart can stay tender, the staying enabling the tenderness. If we have such a heart we can hear the word of mercy and consolation, "Because thine heart wast tender and thou hast humbled thyself before the LORD . . . I also have heard thee, saith the LORD."[46] A reliably tender heart is the supreme good.

Saint John Houghton

Many are the witnesses to this staying of the heart in what abides: people who have gone before us in the way of fidelity to the eternal, who show us it can really be done. One who gave very direct witness is the English Carthusian martyr, St John Houghton, Prior of London. Already the Carthusian life itself is a witness to the eternal: the separation is such that the monks

---

43 *Nicholas of Cusa,* 46.   44 Eph 4:15.   45 1 Thes 3:12–13.
46 2 Kgs 22:19.

can confidently make their own the Lord's saying, "I receive not honour from men."[47] I paid a visit once to the "Grande Chartreuse," the mother house of the order. There is a place where visitors can go to find out about their life. The actual house is some distance from this. You can walk there, but there is no possibility of going in. You can't see a Carthusian monk. Yet you can see the real presence in the monastery: behind securely thick glass is displayed (as I remember) a ciborium containing the Blessed Sacrament. God is exposed to view; the monks not. Silence and solitude reign. There is no openness to the public, but every help to being open to the Eternal. This was the milieu of St John Houghton and his monks. They were asked to assent to the Act of Supremacy making Henry VIII the supreme governor of the Church in England. They prayed for three days and then celebrated a Mass of the Holy Spirit, who gave them their answer. They refused. So they died, as they had lived, for the primacy of the spiritual as embodied and exercised (how worthily is not the issue) by the Pope, the spiritual and not the temporal leader. They chose what abides, not an illusory safety in a life that passes. As they were led to Tyburn, the place of their execution, St Thomas More and his daughter Meg were watching. "Look Meg!" he said, "These blessed Fathers be now as cheerfully going to their deaths as bridegrooms to their marriage!" They were executed on May 4, 1535. The Dominican friar, Anthony Rescius, heard St John Houghton say, just before the executioner cut out his heart, "Good Jesus, what will ye do with my heart?"[48] In other words, St John gave his heart to Jesus. It was an established heart, made strong and tender by his world-overcoming faith in Jesus, the Son of God. God is never outdone in generosity, so we can only suppose that St John received in return the Sacred Heart of Jesus, in which no one and nothing is neglected, and which is supremely stable, supremely tender.

47　Jn 5:41.
48　Cf. *New Catholic Encyclopedia* (New York: McGraw-Hill), vol. 7, 174–75.

Posthumous Philanthropy

There are shelves full of the lives of other such people. They are not simply exemplars to us: we are in communion with them. In God, who is the source of all being, we are one with them. What was said in Chapter 3 about "the oneness where all name is gone" also applies to them. God is our life and since He is the life of all others as well, we are one with those who have gone before. They are "dead" only to this world, for God said to Moses from the burning bush, "I am the God of Abraham, and the God of Isaac, and the God of Jacob" and He is "not the God of the dead, but of the living."[49] In God they live with us still. The witness they gave to the abiding by their endurance in this world to death continues in their witness to the abiding by their endurance in this world after death: by the good they continue to do. Such a one is St Thérèse of Lisieux, who said, "If the good God fulfils my desires, my Heaven will be passed on earth until the end of the world. Yes, I want to pass Heaven doing good on earth. It is not impossible, since in the very heart of the beatific vision the angels watch over us."[50] The following day she added, "The good God would not give me this desire to do good on the earth after my death, if He didn't want to make it happen."[51] There are many such deeds recorded. One that particularly appeals is the healing from blindness, as a child, of Edith Piaf the singer who gave us "La vie en rose" and "Je ne regrette rien." As in her mortal life on earth, so in her posthumous life, St Thérèse did things "pour faire plaisir" — to give pleasure.

---

49 Mt 22:32.
50 "Si le bon Dieu exauce mes désirs, ma Ciel se passera sur la terre jusqu'à la fin du monde. Oui, je veux passer mon Ciel à faire du bien sur la terre. C'est n'est pas impossible, puisqu'au sein même de la vision béatifique les Anges veillent sur nous," from *Thérèse de L'Enfant-Jésus*, 1050.
51 "Le bon Dieu ne me donnerait pas ce désir de faire du bien sur la terre après ma mort, s'il ne voulait pas le realiser," from *Thérèse de L'Enfant-Jé-sus*, 1051.

Eternal Life

Both these kinds of witness from the saints, that given before and that given after death, point us to the ultimate fruit of abiding: "If that which ye have heard from the beginning shall remain (μείνῃ / *meine*) in you, ye also shall continue (μενεῖτε / *meneite*) in the Son, and in the Father. And this is the promise that he hath promised us, even eternal life."[52] The word rendered "continue" is the same as that for "remain" and could also be translated as "abide" or "dwell" or "stay." It is the word that has been tracked throughout this book. The message is that if we allow the Lord to abide with us we have abiding and eternal life. The promise is of "a city which hath foundations, whose builder and maker is God."[53] This city is the "Jerusalem which is above" and "which is mother of us all."[54] We know it already obscurely in the tenderness we have for one another. We are promised an awakening to the ultimate civility: "At that day ye shall know that I am in my Father, and ye in me and I in you,"[55] the mutual indwelling of relations that transcend the spatial and include "us all." It is a promise that we shall abide as God abides, for "He that doeth the will of God abideth for ever."[56] The sharing of God's will in this life is the sharing of His life in the next.

An Eternal Perspective

The way to this abiding is living with an eternal perspective, looking "not at the things that are seen, but at the things which are not seen: for the things which are seen are temporal; but the things which are unseen are eternal."[57] If we see things now as they will look from our eternal abode, the heavenly Jerusalem, then troubles are lightened and accepting the will of God becomes not a frustration of earthly hope but an enabling of heavenly hope. That is not really a deferral of enjoyment if the Lord abides with us now. It is rather an actualization of heavenly

52 1 Jn 2:24–25.   53 Heb 11:10.   54 Gal 4:26.   55 Jn 14:20.
56 1 Jn 2:17.   57 2 Cor 4:18.

living here and now. It transforms our life, drawing the sting of what might poison or embitter it, as the confidence of the hymn-writer[58] testifies:

> I fear no foe, with Thee at hand to bless;
> Ills have no weight, and tears no bitterness;
> Where is death's sting? Where, grave, thy victory?
> I triumph still, if Thou abide with me.

To live like this is to know that "our light affliction, which is but for a moment, worketh for us a far more exceeding and eternal weight of glory."[59] It is to know that only what abides really matters, for "if any man's work abide which he hath built thereupon, he shall receive a reward,"[60] a reward of eternal and abiding joy. Such knowledge leads to the understanding St Paul had gained when he wrote, "I have learned, in whatsoever state I am, therewith to be content."[61] It is the polar opposite to the mind-set of the old woman in the story who lived in a vinegar bottle and was offered three wishes by a good fairy. She claimed the first to transport herself to a large and airy mansion. She found it unsatisfactorily draughty and used her second wish to find new accommodation. That too was deemed wanting and her final wish was to return to the vinegar bottle, which goes to show that bitterness of spirit is a choice. The Lord can set us free from it if we invite him to abide in our vinegar bottle. He has already tasted for us vinegar "mingled with gall."[62] This freedom He gives us is not a freedom from trouble or perplexity, but from the spirit of defeat. With Saint Paul we can say, "We are troubled on every side, yet not distressed; we are perplexed, but not in despair; Persecuted, but not forsaken; cast down, but not destroyed."[63] This "spirit of faith"[64] comes from "bearing about in the body the dying of the Lord Jesus, that the life also of Jesus might be made manifest in our body."[65] It is a confidence about

58 Henry Francis Lyte.   59 2 Cor 4:17.   60 1 Cor 3:14.   61 Phil 4:11.
62 Mt 27:34.   63 2 Cor 4:8–9.   64 2 Cor 4:13.   65 2 Cor 4:10.

the "far more exceeding and eternal weight of glory" that comes from sharing the life of Jesus.

We can live for this promise, this reward, this glory for we have the means to touch it now: "now abideth faith, hope, charity, these three; but the greatest of these is charity."[66] Through these abiding virtues we touch God, who is our eternal and abiding life. Faith enables our intellect to know Him; hope is the handle by which our memory holds Him; charity moves our will to embrace Him. Our embracing of what abides is the continuing exercise of charity which "suffereth long . . . beareth all things . . . endureth all things."[67] Enduring, we win what endures; we have the life in abundance that Jesus came to bring us,[68] for "the world passeth away, and the lust thereof: but he that doeth the will of God abideth for ever."[69] If the passing things of this world fail to please, we know that we "have in heaven a better and enduring substance"[70] where there "are many mansions" and "a place" is prepared for us.[71] The "mansions" are μοναι (*monai*): abodes, the noun corresponding to the verb that has been the theme of this book. The Lord makes this preparation so "that where I am, there ye may be also." He offers us a place in the burning bush whence "I AM THAT I AM"[72] is spoken; He gives us the motherhood of Mary whom the bush prefigures; He prepares a nuptial chamber for us, His Bride, the Church.

Dante's Journey

In Dante's poetic rendering of the journey to this "place" the penultimate stage is the seventh heaven, specially associated with contemplatives and the sphere of Saturn, the planet for which Saturday is named. According to the first Chancellor of Oxford University, Robert Grosseteste, Saturn's sphere is the most luminous, being the nearest to the light promulgated by the divine command, "Let there be light."[73] Concomitantly, it

66 1 Cor 13:13.   67 1 Cor 13:4,7.   68 Cf. Jn 10:10.   69 1 Jn 2:17.
70 Heb 10:34.   71 Jn 14:2.   72 Ex 3:14.
73 Gn 1:3. See Bucklow, *Alchemy of Paint*, 129–30.

is the sphere furthest from the earth where it is relatively dark and difficult to know with clarity. The journey to the seventh heaven, then, is the journey to enlightenment. That corresponds with Saturn as a figure of age and wisdom and also with the color of the rust associated with its metal, lead. This is white, the brightest metallic rust.[74] Saturn was also known as Kronos, the Greek god of time. Its sphere therefore is the one where time, so to speak, "begins." That is reflected in the myth of Saturn eating his children as time devours all that happens within it.[75] All that is within the sphere of Saturn, which includes all the other spheres with earth at their center, is subject to time. The journey to that sphere is the journey to the outermost limit of time. It is a returning to God from whom we came. The week therefore, ending with Saturday, is mimetic of a human life, the proper fulfillment of which is enlightenment. I hope that this, literary if not literal, week has brought you nearer to the light.

Beyond this sphere where there is fullness of light and wisdom there is only eternity, that which truly abides. Dante captures poetically what it is to be within touching distance of the eternally abiding. In *Paradiso* he sees the souls of the blessed, "a hundred little spheres which beautified each other with their mutual beams" (*cento sperule che 'nseme/ più s'abbellivan con mutuï rai*). One of them, St Benedict, explains that they were "men of contemplation" (*contemplanti/ uomini*) and introduces two of his brothers who "stayed their feet within the cloisters and kept steadfast hearts" (*dentro ai chiostri/ fermer li piedi e tennero il cor saldo*).[76] My prayer, dear reader, is that although you may not be cloistered, you will have a steadfast heart, established in that which endures, so that you may reach what abides eternally. "There all we long for is perfect, ripe and whole" (*Ivi è perfetta, matura ed intera/ ciascuna disïanza.*)[77] You will reach it

---

74 Bucklow, *Alchemy of Paint*, 133.   75 Bucklow, *Alchemy of Paint*, 143-46.
76 *Paradiso*, XXII lines 23-24, 46-47, 50-51 in *Dante, The Divine Comedy 3: Paradiso*, 316-19.
77 *Paradiso*, XXII, lines 64-65, 318-19.

through Him who is "the way, the truth, and the life."[78] His final word in John's gospel is "Follow thou me,"[79] inviting a continuation of the adventure of following Jesus presented in its first chapter.[80] Respond steadfastly. Stay with Him; He will stay with you. Tenderly.

78 Jn 14:6.   79 Jn 21:22.   80 Jn 1:37.

ACKNOWLEDGEMENTS

I am most grateful to the following who have read early drafts of this book and helped me to clarify and develop its content: Sam Davidson, Julian Davies, Blake Everitt, Matthew Jarvis O.P., Nicholas King S.J., Martin McGee O.S.B., Xavier Perrin O.S.B, Huw Robinson, Julia Trahair, Andrew, Joe & Katherine Tulloch, Andrew Wye.

Made in the USA
Columbia, SC
15 November 2022